United States Government Accountability Office

Report to Congressional Committees

I0417066

July 2013

INTERNAL CONTROLS

SEC Should Consider Requiring Companies to Disclose Whether They Obtained an Auditor Attestation

GAO Highlights

Highlights of GAO-13-582, a report to congressional committees

INTERNAL CONTROLS

SEC Should Consider Requiring Companies to Disclose Whether They Obtained an Auditor Attestation

Why GAO Did This Study

Section 404(b) of the Sarbanes-Oxley Act requires a public company to have its independent auditor attest to and report on management's internal control over financial reporting; this is known as the auditor attestation requirement. In July 2010, the Dodd-Frank Wall Street Reform and Consumer Protection Act exempted companies with less than $75 million in public float from the auditor attestation requirement. The act mandated that GAO examine the impact of the permanent exemption on the quality of financial reporting by small public companies and on investors. This report discusses (1) how the number of financial statement restatements compares between exempt and nonexempt companies (i.e., those with $75 million or more in public float), (2) the costs and benefits of complying with the attestation requirement, and (3) what is known about the extent to which investor confidence is affected by compliance with the auditor attestation requirement. GAO analyzed financial restatements and audit fees data; surveyed 746 public companies with a response rate of 25 percent; interviewed regulatory officials and others; and reviewed laws, surveys, and studies.

What GAO Recommends

GAO recommends that SEC consider requiring public companies, where applicable, to explicitly disclose whether they obtained an auditor attestation of their internal controls. SEC responded that investors could determine attestation status from available information. But without clear disclosure, investors may misinterpret a company's status; therefore, this warrants SEC's further consideration.

View GAO-13-582. For more information, contact A. Nicole Clowers at (202) 512-8678 or clowersa@gao.gov.

What GAO Found

Since the implementation of the auditor attestation requirement of the Sarbanes-Oxley Act of 2002 (Sarbanes-Oxley Act), companies exempt from the requirement have had more financial restatements (a company's revision of publicly reported financial information) than nonexempt companies, and the percentage of exempt companies restating generally has exceeded that of nonexempt companies. Exempt and nonexempt companies restated their financial statements for similar reasons (e.g., revenue recognition and expenses), and the majority of these restatements produced a negative effect on the companies' financial statements.

Percentage of Exempt and Nonexempt Companies That Restated Their Financial Statements, 2005 to 2011

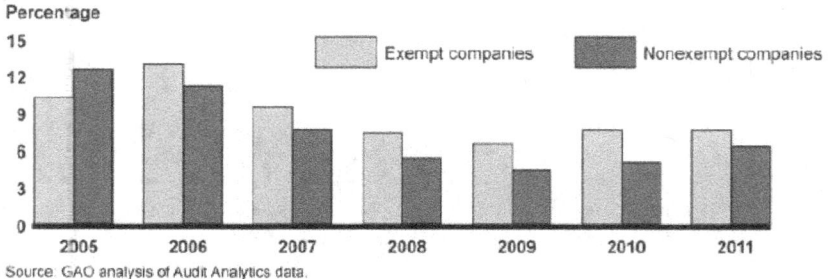

Source: GAO analysis of Audit Analytics data.

Note: Nonexempt companies first complied with the Section 404(b) requirement for their first fiscal year ending on or after November 15, 2004. Exempt companies never had to comply with the requirement.

Views on the costs and benefits of auditor attestation vary among companies and others. Although companies and others reported that the costs associated with compliance can be significant, especially for smaller companies, GAO's and others' analyses show that these costs have declined for companies of all sizes since 2004. Companies and others reported benefits of compliance, such as improved internal controls and reliability of financial reports. However, measuring whether auditor attestation compliance costs outweigh the benefits is difficult and views among companies and others were mixed as to whether the costs exceeded the benefits of compliance.

A majority of empirical studies GAO reviewed suggest that compliance with the auditor attestation requirement has a positive impact on investor confidence in the quality of financial reports. Some interviewees said the independent scrutiny of a company's internal controls is an important investor protection safeguard. The Securities and Exchange Commission (SEC) does not require exempt companies to disclose in their annual report whether they voluntarily obtained an auditor attestation. SEC officials said it is not common for SEC to require a company to disclose voluntary compliance with requirements from which it is exempt. However, federal securities laws require companies to disclose relevant information to investors to aid in their investment decisions. Although information on auditor attestation status is available to investors, requiring a company to explicitly state whether it has obtained an auditor attestation on internal controls could increase transparency and investor protection.

_____ **United States Government Accountability Office**

Contents

Figures

July 3, 2013

The Honorable Tim Johnson
Chairman
The Honorable Mike Crapo
Ranking Member
Committee on Banking, Housing, and Urban Affairs
United States Senate

The Honorable Jeb Hensarling
Chairman
The Honorable Maxine Waters
Ranking Member
Committee on Financial Services
House of Representatives

Public and investor confidence in the accuracy, reliability, and
transparency of companies' financial reporting is critical to the effective
functioning of U.S. capital markets. In response to a series of high-profile
corporate accounting scandals that resulted in substantial losses to
investors at the start of the last decade, Congress passed the Sarbanes-
Oxley Act of 2002 (Sarbanes-Oxley Act).[1] The act introduced major
reforms to public company financial reporting and auditing that were
intended to, among other things, improve the reliability of financial
reporting and enhance audit quality. Effective internal controls are a key
focus of these reforms. In particular, Section 404(b) of the act—the
auditor attestation requirement—requires that each public company's
independent auditor annually attest to and report on management's
assessment of the effectiveness of the company's internal control over
financial reporting.[2] The auditor determines whether any material
weaknesses exist as of year-end.

---

[1]Pub. L. No. 107-204, 116 Stat. 745 (2002).

[2]Section 404(b) applies to companies required to file reports with the Securities and
Exchange Commission (SEC) under the Securities Exchange Act of 1934. *Id* at § 404(a).
Registered investment companies and asset-backed issuers generally are exempt from
Section 404(b). *See* Management's Report on Internal Control Over Financial Reporting
and Certification of Disclosure in Exchange Act Reports, 68 Fed. Reg. 36,636 (June 18,
2003).

The auditor attestation requirement has been subject to much debate since its inception. Congress, business groups, regulators, consumer, investor and auditing groups, and academics have debated the need for small public companies (generally considered to be public companies with a publicly available stock value of less than $75 million) to comply with the auditor attestation requirement. Opponents of the requirement argue that compliance is too costly, especially for small public companies. In contrast, proponents of the requirement argue that, generally, small public companies lack adequate internal controls and restate their financial statements—that is, revise their financial statements to correct accounting errors—more often than large companies. Therefore, they argue, the requirement provides an important investor protection safeguard by ensuring independent scrutiny of a company's financial reporting process.

The Dodd-Frank Wall Street Reform and Consumer Protection Act (Dodd-Frank Act) Section 989G, amended the Sarbanes-Oxley Act so that Section 404(b) does not apply with respect to "any audit report prepared for an issuer that is neither a 'large accelerated filer' nor an 'accelerated filer' as those terms are defined" by the Securities and Exchange Commission (SEC).[3] By adding Section 404(c) to the Sarbanes-Oxley Act, Section 989G permanently exempted smaller issuers from the requirement to obtain an auditor's attestation on management's assessment of the company's effectiveness of internal control over financial reporting.[4] At the time of enactment in 2010, Section 989G affected about 5,500 small public companies, representing about 61

---

[3]Pub. L. No. 111-203, § 989G(a), 124 Stat. 1376, 1948 (2010). SEC refers to small public companies and large public companies as nonaccelerated filers and accelerated filers, respectively, and uses a public float measurement to determine the category of filer. Although the term "nonaccelerated filer" is not defined in SEC rules, it refers to a reporting company that does not meet the definition of either an "accelerated filer" or a "large accelerated filer" under the Securities Exchange Act of 1934 Rule 12b-2. 17 C.F.R. § 240.12b-2. An accelerated filer generally is a company that has been public for at least 12 months and, among other things, had at least $75 million but less than $700 million in public float as of the last business day of its most recently completed second fiscal quarter and filed at least one annual report with SEC. A large accelerated filer generally is a company that has been public for at least 12 months and, among other things, had a public float of $700 million or more as of the last business day of its most recently completed second fiscal quarter and filed at least one annual report with SEC. SEC defines public float as the worldwide aggregate market value of voting and nonvoting common equity held by nonaffiliates of the filer.

[4]§ 989G(a).

percent of all public companies, by exempting them from the requirement.[5]

Section 989I of the Dodd-Frank Act mandated us to study and report on the impact of the permanent exemption on the quality of financial reporting by smaller public companies and on investors.[6] This report discusses: (1) how the number of financial statement restatements compares between exempt and nonexempt companies; (2) the costs and benefits for nonexempt companies and exempt companies that voluntarily comply with the auditor attestation requirement; and (3) what is known about the extent to which investor confidence in the integrity of financial statements is affected by whether or not companies comply with the auditor attestation requirement. For the purposes of this report, we define exempt companies as those with less than $75 million in public float (nonaccelerated filers) and nonexempt companies as those with $75 million or more in public float (accelerated filers).

To identify the number of financial statement restatements (referred to as financial restatements) and trends, we analyzed data from Audit Analytics' Restatement database, which contains company information (such as assets, revenues, restatements, market capitalization, location, and industry classification code) for 2005 through 2011.[7] We identified 6,436 financial restatements by 4,536 public companies, 2,834 of which were exempt companies.[8] We used Audit Analytics' 69 classifications to classify the type of financial restatements into six categories: core expenses (i.e., ongoing operating expenses), noncore expenses (i.e., nonoperating or nonrecurring expenses), revenue recognition, reclassifications and disclosures, underlying events (i.e., accounting for mergers or acquisitions), and other (e.g., restatements related to

---

[5]See Securities and Exchange Commission, *Study and Recommendations on Section 404(b) of the Sarbanes-Oxley Act of 2002 For Issuers with Public Float Between $75 and $250 Million* (Washington, D.C.: April 2011).

[6]§ 989I(a)-(b).

[7]Audit Analytics is an online market intelligence service that provides information on SEC registrants. Audit Analytics maintains a proprietary database containing information from the filings public companies submit to SEC, such as audit fees, audit opinions, and financial restatements.

[8]The number of financial restatements exceeds the number of public companies issuing financial restatements because some of these companies restated their financial statements more than once.

GAO-13-582 Auditor Attestation on Internal Controls

pensions and any other issues identified in the restatement).[9] To identify audit costs of compliance, we analyzed data from Audit Analytics' Auditor Opinion database, which contains auditors' report information, including audit fees, nonaudit fees, auditor name, audit opinions, revenues, and company size, for 2005 through 2011. Our analyses of audit costs do not include 2012 data because some of the data for small companies were incomplete as we concluded our analysis. According to Audit Analytics, the incomplete data was often due to the fact that the small companies had not yet filed the relevant information with SEC. In addition, although 2012 restatement data are available, we were unable to conduct some of our analyses of restatements for 2012 because of incomplete 2012 small-company data in the Auditor Opinion database. We tested samples of the Audit Analytics database information and found it to be reliable for our purposes.

To obtain information on large and small public companies' experiences with the costs and benefits of complying with the auditor attestation requirement and the extent to which investor confidence in the integrity of financial statements is affected by companies' compliance with the requirement (referred to as auditor attestation status), we identified a population of 4,053 companies that fit within the scope of our review. To define the population, we obtained a list of all publicly traded companies for calendar years 2004 through 2011 from Audit Analytics. We stratified the population into three strata by first identifying the nonaccelerated filers that voluntarily complied with the integrated audit requirement in any year from 2004 through 2011. We excluded from our population any exempt company that did not obtain an auditor attestation of its internal controls and then stratified the remaining companies into accelerated filers and large accelerated filers.[10] We surveyed all nonaccelerated filers that

---

[9]Susan Scholz, *The Changing Nature and Consequences of Public Company Financial Restatements: 1997-2006*, a special report prepared at the request of the Department of the Treasury, April 2008. Five of the six categories are based on the classification scheme developed by academics Zoe-Vonna Palmrose and Susan Scholz. The remaining category ("other") was developed by GAO and comprises financial restatements that were not included in one of the other categories.

[10]To identify accelerated filers and large accelerated filers, we relied upon the companies' SEC filing status, which is based on public float. In instances in which companies did not disclose their filing status, we relied upon the companies' market capitalization, as reported in the Audit Analytics database, to make an independent determination of likely filing status. Market capitalization is defined as the total dollar market value of all of a firm's outstanding shares and is calculated by multiplying a firm's outstanding shares by the current market price of one share.

voluntarily complied as well as a random sample of both strata of accelerated filers for a total survey population of 746 companies. We received valid responses from 195 companies. The weighted response rate for this survey, which accounts for the differential sampling fractions within each strata, was 25 percent. All percentage estimates presented in this report have a margin of error of plus or minus 15 percentage points or fewer, and all estimates of averages have a relative margin of error of plus or minus 20 percent or less, unless otherwise noted.

For all three objectives, we interviewed representatives of small public companies, regulatory bodies (SEC and Public Company Accounting Oversight Board (PCAOB)), trade associations (representing individual and institutional investors, accounting firms, financial analysts and investment professionals, and financial executives), industry experts, a large pension fund, a credit rating agency, and academics knowledgeable about accounting issues. We also reviewed relevant academic, industry, and SEC research studies and surveys.[11] Appendix I contains a more detailed description of our scope and methodology.

We conducted this performance audit from May 2012 to July 2013 in accordance with generally accepted government auditing standards. Those standards require that we plan and perform the audit to obtain sufficient, appropriate evidence to provide a reasonable basis for our findings and conclusions based on our audit objectives. We believe that the evidence obtained provides a reasonable basis for our findings and conclusions based on our audit objectives.

Background

Internal control generally serves as a first line of defense for public companies in safeguarding assets and preventing and detecting errors and fraud. Internal control is defined as a process, effected by an entity's board of directors, management, and other personnel, designed to provide reasonable assurance regarding the achievement of the following objectives: (1) effectiveness and efficiency of operations; (2) reliability of financial reporting; and (3) compliance with laws and regulations.[12]

---

[11]See the bibliography for a detailed list of sources reviewed.

[12]COSO, Internal Control – Integrated Framework, 1992, 1994, and 2013. The "reliability of financial reporting" objective is the objective that is relevant for purposes of Section 404 and the SEC's implementing rules.

Internal control over financial reporting is further defined in the SEC regulations implementing Section 404 of the Sarbanes-Oxley Act.[13] These regulations define internal control over financial reporting as a means of providing reasonable assurance regarding the reliability of financial reporting and the preparation of financial statements, including those policies and procedures that:

- pertain to the maintenance of records that, in reasonable detail, accurately and fairly reflect the transactions and dispositions of the assets of the company;

- provide reasonable assurance that transactions are recorded as necessary to permit preparation of financial statements in conformity with generally accepted accounting principles, and that receipts and expenditures of the company are being made only in accordance with authorizations of management and directors of the company; and

- provide reasonable assurance regarding prevention or timely detection of unauthorized acquisition, use, or disposition of the company's assets that could have a material effect on the financial statements.[14]

Regulators regard an effective internal control system as a foundation for high-quality financial reporting by companies. Title IV, Section 404 of the Sarbanes-Oxley Act, aims to help protect investors by, among other things, improving the accuracy, reliability, and transparency of corporate financial reporting and disclosures. Section 404 has the following two key sections:

- Section 404(a) requires company management to state its responsibility for establishing and maintaining an adequate internal control structure and procedures for financial reporting and assess the effectiveness of its internal control over financial reporting in each annual report filed with SEC.[15] In 2007, SEC issued guidance for

---

[13]Management's Report on Internal Control Over Financial Reporting and Certification of Disclosure in Exchange Act Reports, 68 Fed. Reg. 36636 (June 18, 2003) (amending 17 C.F.R. §§ 210, 228, 229, 240, 249, 270, and 274).

[14]*Id.*

[15]Pub. L. No. 107-204, § 404(a), 116 Stat. 745, 789 (2010) (codified as amended at 15 U.S.C. § 7262).

management regarding its report on internal control over financial reporting.[16]

- Section 404(b) requires the firms that serve as external auditors for public companies to provide an opinion on the internal control assessment made by the companies' management regarding the effectiveness of the company's internal control over financial reporting as of year-end.[17] In 2007, PCAOB issued Auditing Standard No. 5, which contains the requirements that apply when an auditor is engaged to perform an audit of management's assessment of the effectiveness of internal control over financial reporting.[18]

While management is responsible for the implementation of an effective internal control process, the external auditor obtains reasonable assurance to provide an opinion on the effectiveness of a company's internal control over financial reporting through an independent audit. Investors need to know that the financial statements on which they make investment decisions are reliable. The auditor attestation process involves the external auditor's testing and evaluation of the company's internal control over financial reporting and relevant documentation in order to provide an opinion on the effectiveness of the company's internal control over financial reporting as of year-end; a company's internal control over financial reporting cannot be considered effective if one or more material weaknesses exist.[19]

Auditor attestation of the effectiveness of internal control over financial reporting has been required for public companies with a public float of

---

[16]*Commission Guidance Regarding Management's Report on Internal Control over Financial Reporting Under Section 13(a) or 15(d) of the Securities Exchange Act of 1934,* Interpretation, SEC Release No. 33-8810 (June 20, 2007).

[17]§ 404(b).

[18]Auditing Standard No. 5, *An Audit of Internal Control Over Financial Reporting That Is Integrated with an Audit of Financial Statements* (PCAOB 2007).

[19]SEC and PCAOB define a material weakness as a deficiency, or combination of deficiencies, in internal control over financial reporting such that there is a reasonable possibility that a material misstatement of the firm's annual or interim financial statements will not be prevented or detected on a timely basis. *See* SEC Regulation S-X, 17 C.F.R. § 210.1-02(a)(4); Auditing Standard No. 5.

$75 million or more (accelerated filers) since 2004.[20] However, SEC delayed implementing the auditor attestation for public companies with less than $75 million in public float (nonaccelerated filers) several times from the original compliance date of April 15, 2005, to June 15, 2010, in response to concerns about compliance costs and management and auditor preparedness.[21] On July 21, 2010, the Dodd-Frank Act permanently exempted nonaccelerated filers from the auditor attestation requirement.[22] The Dodd-Frank Act did not exempt nonaccelerated filers from Section 404(a) of the Sarbanes-Oxley Act (management's assessment of internal controls). See table 1 for final compliance dates for internal control over financial reporting by issuer filer status.

---

[20]Management's Report on Internal Control Over Financial Reporting and Certification of Disclosure in Exchange Act Reports, 68 Fed. Reg. at 36,647.

[21]GAO, *Community Banks and Credit Unions: Impact of the Dodd-Frank Act Depends Largely on Future Rule Makings*, GAO-12-881 (Washington, D.C.: Sep. 13, 2012).

[22]Pub. L. No. 111-203, § 989G(a), 124 Stat. 1376, 1948 (2010) (codified at 15 U.S.C.§7262) (amending Sarbanes-Oxley Act). SEC amended its rules and forms to conform to Section 404(c) of the Sarbanes-Oxley Act, as added by Section 989G of the Dodd-Frank Act. *See* Internal Control Over Financial Reporting in Exchange Act Periodic Reports of Non-Accelerated Filers, 75 Fed. Reg. 57,385 (Sept. 21, 2010). Section 404(c) provides that Section 404(b) of the Sarbanes-Oxley Act shall not apply with respect to any audit report prepared for an issuer that is neither an accelerated filer nor a large accelerated filer as defined in Rule 12b–2 under the Securities Exchange Act of 1934. Pub. L. No. 107-204, § 404(c), 116 Stat. 745, 789 (2010) (codified as amended at 15 U.S.C. § 7262). Additionally, the Jumpstart Our Business Startups Act ("JOBS Act") also exempted emerging growth companies, defined generally as issuers with less than $1 billion in annual gross revenue, from the auditor attestation requirement of Section 404(b) as long as the issuer retains emerging growth company status, which is subject to four conditions. Among other conditions, an issuer will ordinarily no longer retain emerging growth company status at the end of the fiscal year in which the fifth anniversary of its initial public offering of common equity securities occurs. Pub. L. No. 112-106, § 103, 126 Stat. 306, 310 (2012). In addition, our study did not specifically address the impact of this JOBS Act exemption on the number of exempt companies, the number of restatements by exempt companies, the auditor attestation practices of newly public companies or investor perception of the reliability of financial statements of emerging growth companies.

Table 1: Sarbanes-Oxley Act Section 404 Requirements Compliance Dates by Filer Status Set by SEC

		Compliance dates for internal control over financial reporting requirements	
	Issuer filer status	Management's report on internal controls and effectiveness	External auditor's attestation report on internal controls and effectiveness
U.S. issuer	Large accelerated filer or accelerated filer ($75 million or more in public float)	Annual reports filed with SEC for fiscal years ending on or after November 15, 2004	Annual reports filed with SEC for fiscal years ending on or after November 15, 2004
	Nonaccelerated filer (less than $75 million in public float)	Annual reports filed with SEC for fiscal years ending on or after December 15, 2007	Permanently exempted by Dodd-Frank Act on July 21, 2010
Foreign private issuer	Large accelerated filer ($700 million or more in public float)	Annual reports filed with SEC for fiscal years ending on or after July 15, 2006	Annual reports filed with SEC for fiscal years ending on or after July 15, 2006
	Accelerated filer ($75 million or more and less than $700 million in public float)	Annual reports filed with SEC for fiscal years ending on or after July 15, 2006	Annual reports filed with SEC for fiscal years ending on or after July 15, 2007
	Nonaccelerated filer (less than $75 million in public float)	Annual reports filed with SEC for fiscal years ending on or after December 15, 2007	Permanently exempted by Dodd-Frank Act on July 21, 2010
Newly public company (U.S. or foreign private issuer)	Large accelerated filer or accelerated filer ($75 million or more in public float)	Second annual report filed with SEC following company's initial public offering	Second annual report filed with SEC following company's initial public offering
	Nonaccelerated filer (less than $75 million in public float)	Second annual report filed with SEC following company's initial public offering	Permanently exempted by Dodd-Frank Act on July 21, 2010

Sources: GAO and SEC.

Note: Foreign private issuers are generally foreign companies that have a relatively lesser degree of U.S. share ownership or U.S. business contacts. SEC has adopted special rules applicable to foreign private issuers that are designed to recognize international and home jurisdiction. 17 C.F.R. § 240.3b-4; 17 C.F.R. § 230.405.

The number of exempt companies exceeded the number of nonexempt companies in each year from 2005 through 2011 (see table 2). According to our analysis of Audit Analytics data, the number of exempt companies fluctuated and ultimately declined from 6,333 in 2005 to 5,459 in 2011 (13.8 percent during that period). The number of nonexempt companies also fluctuated and ultimately declined from 4,256 in 2005 to 3,671 in 2011(13.7 percent).

Table 2: Number of Exempt and Nonexempt Companies, 2005-2011

Year	Number of exempt companies	Number of nonexempt companies
2005	6,333	4,256
2006	5,858	4,455
2007	5,530	4,437
2008	5,915	4,166
2009	6,285	3,697
2010	6,166	3,586
2011	5,459	3,671

Source: GAO analysis of Audit Analytics data.

Note: The number of exempt companies includes companies that voluntarily complied with the auditor attestation requirement. Company estimates in the table do not include subsidiaries of a public company, registered investment companies, or asset-backed securities issuers. Exempt companies are nor accelerated filers, including smaller reporting companies. For our purposes, we grouped companies that did not disclose their filing status but whose market capitalization was less than $75 million with exempt companies. For example, companies that did not disclose their filing status include Canadian Form 40-F filers. We used market capitalization as a proxy for public float in these instances because the Audit Analytics database did not contain information on companies' public float. Nonexempt companies are accelerated filers and large accelerated filers. For our purposes, we grouped companies that did not disclose their filing status but whose market capitalization was equal to or greater than $75 million with nonexempt companies. We excluded companies that did not disclose their filing status and that did not have a reported market capitalization.

SEC and PCAOB have issued regulations, standards, and guidance to implement the Sarbanes-Oxley Act. In 2007, in response to companies' concerns about implementation costs, SEC provided implementation guidance to company management, and PCAOB issued a new auditing standard to external auditors to make the internal controls audit process more efficient and more cost-effective.[23] SEC's guidance for management in implementing Section 404(a) of Sarbanes-Oxley Act and PCAOB's Auditing Standard No. 5 for external auditors in implementing Section 404(b) of Sarbanes-Oxley Act endorsed a "top-down, risk-based approach" that emphasizes preventing or detecting material misstatements in financial statements by focusing on those risks that are more likely to contribute to such misstatements. These changes were provided to create a more flexible environment where company management and external auditors can scale their internal controls

---

[23]*Commission Guidance Regarding Management's Report on Internal Control Over Financial Reporting Under Section 13(a) or 15(d) of the Securities Exchange Act of 1934,* Interpretation, 72 Fed. Reg. 35,324 (June 27, 2007); and Auditing Standard No. 5, *An Audit of Internal Control Over Financial Reporting That Is Integrated with an Audit of Financial Statements* (PCAOB 2007).

evaluation based on the particular characteristics of a company to reduce costs and to align SEC and PCAOB requirements for evaluating the effectiveness of internal controls.

Both SEC regulations and PCAOB Auditing Standard No. 5 state that management is required to base its assessment of the effectiveness of the company's internal control over financial reporting on a suitable, recognized control framework established by a body of experts that followed due process procedures. Both the SEC guidance and PCAOB's auditing standard cite the Committee of Sponsoring Organizations of the Treadway Commission (COSO) framework as an example of a suitable framework for purposes of Section 404 compliance.[24] In 1992, COSO issued its "Internal Control—Integrated Framework" (the COSO framework) to help businesses and other entities assess and enhance their internal controls. Since that time, the COSO framework has been recognized by regulatory standard setters and others as a comprehensive framework for evaluating internal control, including internal control over financial reporting.[25] The framework consists of five interrelated components: control environment, risk assessment, control activities, information and communication, and monitoring.[26] However, SEC and PCAOB do not mandate the use of any particular framework.

---

[24]COSO was originally formed in 1985 to sponsor the National Commission on Fraudulent Financial Reporting, an independent private-sector initiative that studied the causal factors that can lead to fraudulent financial reporting and developed recommendations for public companies and their independent auditors, SEC and other regulators, and educational institutions.

[25]COSO, *Internal Control – Integrated Framework*, 1992, 1994, and 2013.

[26]On May 14, 2013, COSO issued an update to its 1992 Internal Control-Integrated Framework to: (1) reflect a business environment that is more complex than it was when the original framework was developed; (2) broaden the application of internal control in addressing operations and reporting objectives; and (3) clarify what constitutes effective internal control.

GAO-13-582 Auditor Attestation on Internal Controls

The Percentage of Exempt Companies with Financial Restatements Was Generally Greater Than the Percentage of Nonexempt Companies from 2005 through 2011

Since the implementation of the Sarbanes-Oxley Act, the number and percentage of exempt companies restating their financial statements has generally exceeded the number and percentage of nonexempt companies restating. However, from 2005 through 2011, restatements by exempt companies were generally proportionate to their percentage of our total population. Specifically, on average, almost 64 percent of companies restating were exempt companies and exempt companies made up, on average, 60 percent of our total population. Exempt and nonexempt companies restated their financial statements for similar reasons, and the majority of these restatements produced a negative effect on the companies' financial statements.

Exempt Companies Generally Have Had More Financial Restatements Than Nonexempt Companies

The number of financial statement restatements by exempt and nonexempt companies has generally declined since 2005. As illustrated in figure 1, the number of financial restatements peaked in 2006 for exempt companies and declined gradually until 2011, despite a slight uptick in 2010. The number of restatements peaked in 2005 for nonexempt companies, declined gradually until 2009, and then trended upward for the remaining 2 years of the review period. As we have previously reported, some industry observers noted the financial reporting requirements of the Sarbanes-Oxley Act and PCAOB inspections may have led to a higher than average number of restatements in 2005 and 2006.[27] A 2010 Audit Analytics report noted that some observers attributed the subsequent decline in restatements to a belief that SEC relaxed standards in 2008 relating to materiality of errors and the need to file restatements.[28] The number of financial restatements by exempt companies exceeded the number of financial restatements by nonexempt companies each year from 2005 through 2011. However, although the overall number of financial restatements from 2009 through 2011 remained lower than the prior period, the number of financial restatements by nonexempt companies increased about 23 percent from

---

[27]GAO, *Financial Restatements: Update of Public Company Trends, Market Impacts, and Regulatory Enforcement Activities*, GAO-06-678 (Washington, D.C.: Mar. 5, 2007).

[28]Audit Analytics, *2009 Financial Restatements: A Nine Year Comparison* (Sutton, Mass.: February 2010).

GAO-13-582 Auditor Attestation on Internal Controls

2010 through 2011. The number of financial restatements by exempt companies declined almost 8 percent during the same period.

SEC officials and one market expert with whom we spoke indicated that there is no clear explanation for these restatement trends. They also said that a review of each individual financial restatement would be necessary to determine the reasons for the restatement trends, but they offered a few factors to consider when assessing the trends. In particular, a recent Audit Analytics report found that approximately 57 percent of restatements disclosed in 2011 were defined as revision restatements, the highest level since 2005 (the first full year of the disclosure requirement).[29] According to the report, revision restatements generally do not undermine reliance on past financials and are less disruptive to the market. SEC officials noted that although restatements by nonexempt companies have increased, as illustrated in the Audit Analytics report, they may be less severe as a result of higher numbers of revision restatements, fewer issues per restatement, and a lower cumulative impact on the company's net income. According to our analysis of Audit Analytics data, in 2011, the percentage of restatements that were revision restatements was approximately 62 percent for exempt companies compared to approximately 70 percent for nonexempt companies. SEC officials also suggested that the detection rate of financial restatements could affect restatement trends, especially when looking only at a one or two year period. The officials said that the lag time on detection and the likelihood of detection could be different between exempt and nonexempt companies. Finally, SEC officials said that it is important to consider the nature and severity of restatements.

---

[29]Audit Analytics, *2011 Financial Restatements: An Eleven Year Comparison* (Sutton, Mass.: April 2012). A revision restatement is defined as a restatement contained in a periodic report without prior disclosure in Form 8-K, Item 4.02. SEC requires public companies to disclose a determination that any previously issued financial statements should no longer be relied upon. Additional Form 8-K Disclosure Requirements and Acceleration of Filing Date, 69 Fed. Reg. 15,594 (Mar. 25, 2004). This set of disclosure requirements became effective August 23, 2004. *Id.*

GAO-13-582 Auditor Attestation on Internal Controls

Figure 1: Number of Restatements by Exempt Companies and Nonexempt Companies, 2005-2011

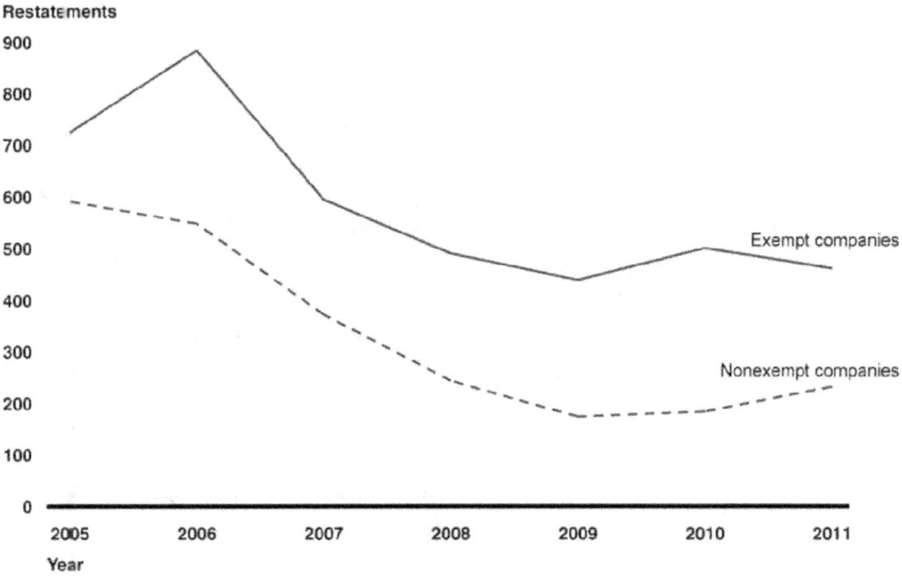

Restatements

Source: GAO analysis of Audit Analytics data.

Note: The data for this table include the number of restatements disclosed in each calendar year from 2005 through 2011.

Except for 2005, the percentage of exempt companies restating their financial statements exceeded the percentage of nonexempt companies restating. From 2006 through 2009, there was a decline in the percentage of restatements for both exempt companies and nonexempt companies. The percentage of exempt companies restating their financial statements rose in 2010 to 7.6 percent and remained constant in 2011 (see fig. 2).[30] At the same time, starting in 2010, the percentage of nonexempt companies restating has been on the increase. In addition, from 2005 to 2011, on average, almost 64 percent of companies restating were exempt companies, which made up 60 percent of our total population.

---

[30]The data reflect the unique number of exempt and nonexempt companies restating in each calendar year, independent of the period or periods being restated. The percentage is calculated by dividing the number of unique restating exempt companies in a given year by the total population of unique exempt companies for that year.

GAO-13-582 Auditor Attestation on Internal Controls

Figure 2: Percentage of Exempt and Nonexempt Companies That Restated Their Financial Statements, 2005-2011

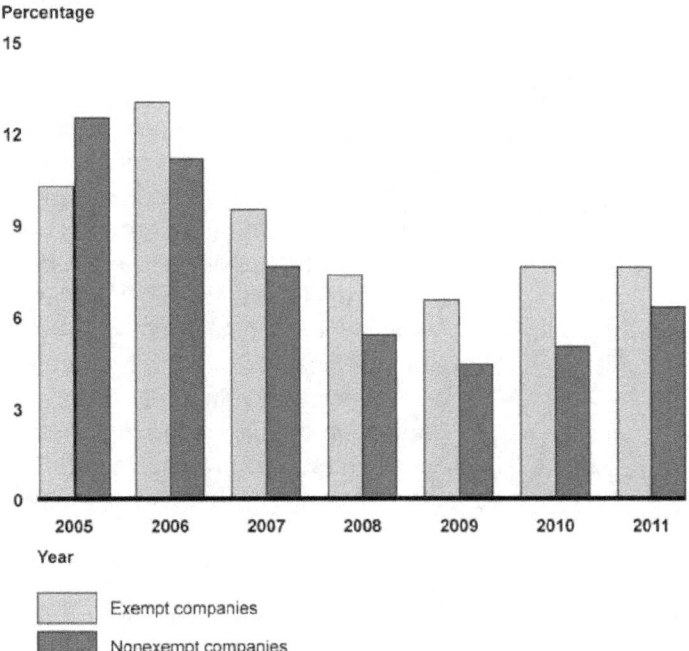

Source: GAO analysis of Audit Analytics data.

Note: The data for this table are based on the proportion of the unique number of exempt and nonexempt companies disclosing a restatement each calendar year divided by the respective populations for fiscal years 2005 through 2011.

Our analysis is generally consistent with a number of studies that have found that exempt companies restate their financial statements at a higher rate than nonexempt companies.[31] These studies suggest that having an auditor attest to the effectiveness of a company's internal control over financial reporting generally reduces the likelihood of financial restatements. For example, in 2009, Audit Analytics found that for companies that did not obtain an auditor attestation and stated that

---

[31]Securities and Exchange Commission, *Study and Recommendations on Section 404(b) of the Sarbanes-Oxley Act of 2002 For Issuers with Public Float Between $75 and $250 Million* (Washington, D.C.: April 2011); Audit Analytics, *Restatements Disclosed by the Two Types of SOX 404 Issuers: (1) Auditor Attestation Filers and (2) Management-Only Report Filers* (Sutton, Mass., November 2009); and A. Nagy, "Section 404 Compliance and Financial Reporting Quality," *Accounting Horizons,* vol. 24, no. 3 (2010).

they had effective internal controls, their financial restatement rate was 46 percent higher than the restatement rate for companies that had obtained an auditor attestation and stated that they had effective internal controls.[32]

Exempt Companies That Voluntarily Complied with Auditor Attestation Issued Fewer Restatements Than Exempt Companies That Did Not

Exempt companies that voluntarily complied with the auditor attestation requirement constitute a small percentage of exempt companies (see table 3). Prior to the passage of the Dodd-Frank Act in July 2010, the number of exempt companies voluntarily complying with the auditor attestation requirement grew 70 percent from 2008 through 2009. Although SEC deferred the requirement for nonaccelerated filers to comply until June 15, 2010, some exempt companies likely voluntarily complied in anticipation of SEC's implementation of the requirement.[33] Nonetheless, in 2009 during the peak compliance period for exempt companies that voluntarily complied, 6.9 percent (435) of a total population of 6,285 exempt companies voluntarily complied with the auditor attestation requirement. According to one academic study, exempt companies that voluntarily comply with the auditor's attestation requirement are more likely than companies that do not comply to have evidence of the superior quality of their internal control over financial reporting and fewer restatements, among other factors.[34]

---

[32]Audit Analytics, *Restatements Disclosed by the Two Types of SOX 404 Issuers: (1) Auditor Attestation Filers and (2) Management-Only Report Filers* (Sutton, Mass., November 2009). Audit Analytics uses SEC data for its analysis, and SEC and PCAOB define internal control over financial reporting as effective if a material weakness does not exist. *See* SEC Regulation S-K, 17 C.F.R § 229.308(a)(3); Auditing Standard No. 5, An Audit of Internal Control Over Financial Reporting that Is Integrated with an Audit of Financial Statements (PCAOB 2007).

[33]Prior to issuing several temporary exemptions from the auditor attestation requirement, SEC issued guidance stating that nonaccelerated (exempt) companies were not required to obtain an auditor's report on internal control over financial reporting until the company filed an annual report for its fiscal year ending on or after April 15, 2005. See Management's Report on Internal Control Over Financial Reporting and Certification of Disclosure in Exchange Act Reports, 68 Fed. Reg. at 36,651.

[34]See K. Brown, P. Pacharn, J. Li, E. Mohammad, F. A. Elayan, and F. Chu, "The Valuation Effect and Motivations of Voluntary Compliance with Auditor's Attestation Under Sarbanes-Oxley Act Section 404 (B)," Working paper, (Jan. 15, 2012).

Table 3: Number of Exempt Companies That Did and Did Not Voluntarily Comply with the Auditor Attestation Requirement and the Percentage of Companies That Filed Restatements, 2005-2011

Year	Exempt companies that did not voluntarily comply			Exempt companies that voluntarily complied			Total exempt companies		
	Total number	Total number restating	Percent restating	Total number	Total number restating	Percent restating	Total number	Total number restating	Percent restating
2005	6,253	643	10.28%	80	7	8.75%	6,333	650	10.26%
2006	5,755	750	13.03	103	12	11.65	5,858	762	13.01
2007	5,370	513	9.55	160	12	7.50	5,530	525	9.49
2008	5,659	418	7.39	256	17	6.64	5,915	435	7.35
2009	5,850	387	6.62	435	24	5.52	6,285	411	6.54
2010	5,816	453	7.79	350	16	4.57	6,166	469	7.61
2011	5,160	392	7.60	299	23	7.69	5,459	415	7.60

Source: GAO analysis of Audit Analytics data.

As table 3 also shows, the percentage of financial restatements by exempt companies that voluntarily complied with the requirement is generally lower than that of exempt companies that did not voluntarily comply. From 2005 through 2011, on average, 7.5 percent of exempt companies that voluntarily complied restated their financial statements compared to 8.9 percent of restating exempt companies that did not voluntarily comply.

Reasons for Financial Restatement and Industry Trends Are Generally Consistent for Both Exempt and Nonexempt Companies

From 2005 through 2011, based on our analysis of Audit Analytics data, the majority of exempt and nonexempt companies that restated their financial statements did so as the result of an accounting rule misapplication.[35] That is, a company revised previously issued public financial information that contained an accounting inaccuracy. To analyze the reasons for financial restatements, we used Audit Analytics' 69 classifications to classify the type of financial restatements into six categories (see table 4): revenue recognition, core expenses, noncore

---

[35]An "accounting rule misapplication" refers to the misapplication of Generally Accepted Accounting Principles.

expenses, reclassifications and disclosures, underlying events, and other.[36]

Table 4: Financial Restatement Category Descriptions

Category	Description
Revenue recognition	Restatements due to improper revenue accounting. This category includes restatements originating from a failure to properly interpret sales contracts for hidden rebate, return, barter, or resale clauses. They may also relate to the treatment of sales returns, credits, and other allowances.
Core expenses	Restatements of companies' ongoing operating expenses. This category includes cost of sales, compensation expenses, lease and depreciation costs, selling, general and administrative expenses, and research and development costs.
Noncore expenses	Restatements that affect net income but do not arise from ongoing operating expenses. This category includes accounting for interest, taxes, and derivatives. It also includes misstatements arising from accounting for nonrecurring events.
Reclassifications and disclosures	Restatements due to improperly classified financial statement items (e.g., current liabilities classified as long-term debt on the balance sheet, or cash flows from operating activities classified as cash flows from financing activities on the statement of cash flows). This category includes restatements that generally revise footnote information.
Underlying events	Restatements due to improper accounting for acquisitions or mergers and issues from problems with foreign affiliates and their related accounting or financial reporting.
Other	Any restatement not covered by the listed categories. This category includes restatements related to pensions and any other issues identified in the restatement

Sources: Zoe-Vonna Palmrose and Susan Scholz and GAO.

Based on our classification, core expenses (i.e., ongoing operating expenses) were the most frequently identified category of restatement for both exempt and nonexempt companies. Specifically, core expenses accounted for 30.2 percent of disclosures by exempt companies and 28.5

---

[36]Five of the six categories are based on the classification scheme developed by academics Zoe-Vonna Palmrose and Susan Scholz. The sixth category ("other") was developed by GAO and comprises financial restatements that were not included in one of the other categories.

percent of disclosures by nonexempt companies from 2005 through 2011 (see fig. 3). Core expenses include cost of sales, compensation expenses, lease and depreciation costs, selling, general and administrative expenses, and research and development costs. Noncore expenses (i.e., nonoperating expenses) were the second most frequently identified reason for restatement across exempt and nonexempt companies during this period. Each of the other reasons for restatements represented less than 20 percent of all restatements by exempt and nonexempt companies during the period.

Figure 3: Reasons for Financial Restatements by Exempt Companies and Nonexempt Companies, 2005-2011

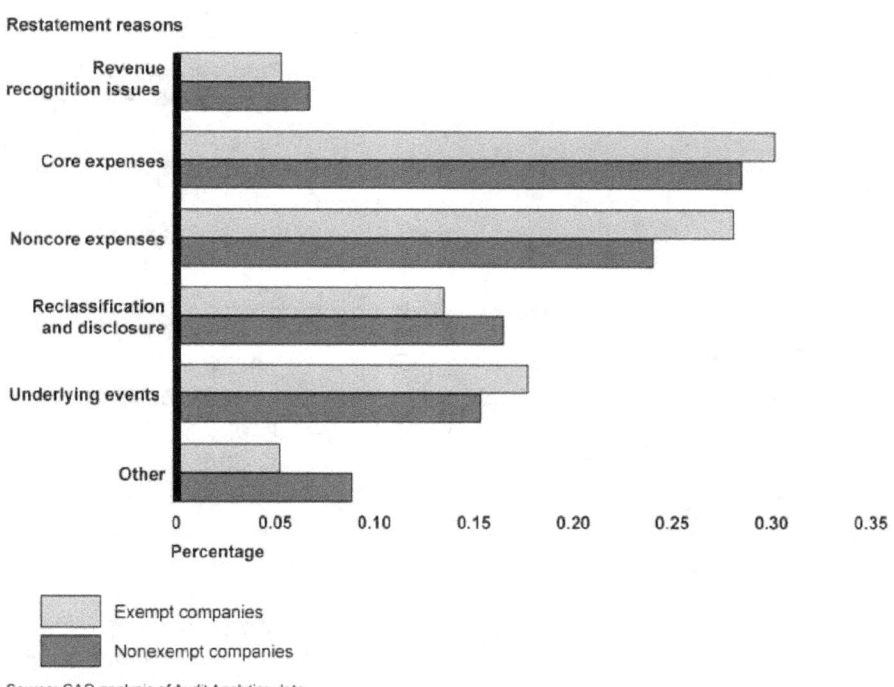

Source: GAO analysis of Audit Analytics data.

From 2005 through 2011, the majority of financial restatements by exempt and nonexempt companies negatively impacted the company's financial statements.[37] Specifically, 87.6 percent of financial restatements by exempt companies resulted in a negative net effect on the financial

---

[37]Audit Analytics' Restatement database includes an assessment of whether the effect on the financial statement is positive or negative.

statements—the income statement, the balance sheet, the statement of cash flows, or the statement of shareholder's equity—of these companies. Similarly, 80.6 percent of financial restatements by nonexempt companies resulted in a negative net effect on the company's financial statements.

The characteristics of exempt and nonexempt companies with financial restatements varied from 2005 through 2011. For example, in terms of industry characteristics, on average, most exempt companies restating were in the manufacturing sector (29.4 percent), followed by agriculture, construction, and mining (14.6 percent). On average, most of the nonexempt companies restating were in the manufacturing sector (29.3 percent), followed by the financial sector (16.6 percent). Further, in 2011, 91.4 percent of nonexempt companies restating compared to 35.3 percent of exempt companies were listed on an exchange.[38] In addition, nonexempt companies had an average financial restatement period that was longer than that of exempt companies.[39] Specifically, from 2005 through 2011, nonexempt companies had an average financial restatement period of 9 quarters compared to an average financial restatement period of almost 6 quarters for exempt companies.

Views on the Costs and Benefits of Auditor Attestation Vary among Companies and Others

Companies and others identified various costs of the auditor attestation requirement. A number of studies and surveys show that since the passage of the Sarbanes-Oxley Act, and especially since the 2007 reforms by SEC and PCAOB, audit costs have declined for companies of all sizes. These studies and surveys also show that these costs, as a percentage of revenues, affect smaller companies disproportionately compared to their larger counterparts. Companies and others also identified benefits of compliance, including stronger internal controls and more transparent and reliable financial reports. However, determining whether auditor attestation compliance costs outweigh the benefits is difficult because many costs and benefits cannot be readily quantified.

---

[38]Companies were listed on the New York Stock Exchange, Nasdaq National Market, Nasdaq Smallcap Market, American Stock Exchange, or were traded in the over-the-counter market.

[39]The financial restatement period is the accounting period (e.g., last 4 quarters) of the previously issued financial statements that contained a material inaccuracy that had to be corrected by filing revised financial statements with SEC.

Auditor Attestation Costs Can Be Significant, Especially for Small Companies, but Costs Are Declining

A number of studies and surveys show that the estimated costs of obtaining an external auditor attestation on internal control over financial reporting are significant for companies of all sizes. Obtaining an auditor attestation incurs both direct and indirect costs, according to one study.[40] Direct costs are expenses incurred to fulfill the auditor attestation requirement, such as the audit fees, external fees paid to outside contractors and vendors that help companies comply with the requirement, salaries of internal staff for hours spent preparing for auditor attestation compliance, and nonlabor expenses (e.g., technology, software, travel, and computers related to compliance). Indirect costs are those costs not directly linked to obtaining the auditor attestation. Two examples of indirect costs cited by one interviewee and one study are the time spent by management in preparing for and addressing auditors' inquiries, which diverts their attention from strategic planning, and the diversion of funds from capital investments to auditor attestation-related expenses.[41]

Audit fees are a significant direct cost of the auditor attestation requirement. Sarbanes-Oxley Act and PCAOB standards require that the financial statement audit and the auditor attestation audit be conducted on an integrated basis.[42] As a result, the auditor attestation is included in the total audit fees—that is, the total amount companies pay to their external auditors to conduct the integrated audit. Audit fees are based on several factors, including but not limited to the scope of an audit, which is a function of a company's complexity and risk; the total effort required by the external auditor to complete the audit; and the risk associated with performing the audit.[43] However, according to SEC's 2011 study and one

---

[40]C. R. Alexander, S. W. Bauguess, G. Bernile, Y. A. Lee, and J. Marietta-Westberg, "The Economic Effects of SOX Section 404 Compliance: A Corporate Insider Perspective," Working paper, (March 2010).

[41]Y. Jahmani and W. A. Dowling, "The Impact of Sarbanes-Oxley Act," *Journal of Business & Economics Research*, vol. 6, no. 10 (2008).

[42]Pub. L. No. 107-204, § 404(b), 116 Stat. 745, 789 (2010) (codified as amended at 15 U.S.C. § 7262); Auditing Standard No. 5, *An Audit of Internal Control Over Financial Reporting That Is Integrated with an Audit of Financial Statements* (PCAOB 2007).

[43]According to PCAOB Auditing Standard No. 8, in an audit of financial statements, audit risk is the risk that the auditor expresses an inappropriate audit opinion when the financial statements are materially misstated, i.e., the financial statements are not presented fairly in conformity with the applicable financial reporting framework. Auditing Standard No. 8, *Audit Risk* (PCAOB 2010).

interviewee, the costs incurred by a company to comply with the auditor attestation requirement generally decline after the initial year.

We analyzed total audit fees as a percentage of revenues from 2005 through 2011 for exempt and nonexempt companies.[44] We found that exempt companies, which tend to be smaller, had higher average total audit costs, measured as a percentage of revenues, compared to nonexempt companies (see table 5). Among exempt companies, the data indicate that exempt companies that do not voluntarily comply with the auditor attestation requirement have (except for 2006) higher average total audit fees as a percentage of revenues than the exempt companies that voluntarily comply. While two academics we contacted about this trend could not provide a definitive explanation, there are many factors beside company size that can affect audit fees.

Table 5: Average Total Audit Fees as a Percentage of Revenues, 2005-2011

Year	Exempt companies that did not voluntarily comply		Exempt companies that voluntarily complied		Nonexempt companies	
	Number of companies	Percentage	Number of companies	Percentage	Number of companies	Percentage
2005	3729	2.93%	50	1.44%	4151	1.40%
2006	2927	2.65	77	3.07	4206	1.41
2007	2370	3.14	111	1.95	4060	1.07
2008	2306	3.19	215	1.16	3967	1.11
2009	2449	3.27	393	2.98	3560	1.33
2010	2546	3.14	322	1.57	3476	0.91
2011	2227	3.41	265	1.22	3556	1.15

Source: GAO analysis of Audit Analytics data.

Note: In calculating the average audit fees as a percentage of revenues, companies in all three categories with less than $150,000 in revenue are excluded.

Our data analysis results are consistent with our previous work on audit fees. Specifically, in 2006, we reported that smaller public companies paid disproportionately higher audit fees compared to larger public

---

[44]SEC defines audit fees as those fees for financial statement audit and review services performed by the auditor to fulfill its responsibility under generally accepted accounting standards or to render an opinion or review report on the financial statements.

companies.[45] Smaller public companies noted that they incur higher audit fees and other costs, such as hiring more staff or paying outside consultants to comply with the internal control provisions of the Sarbanes-Oxley Act. One study noted that historically, these higher audit fees and other costs increased regulatory costs for smaller public companies because regulatory compliance, in general, involves a significant number of fixed costs regardless of the size of a company. Thus, smaller companies with lower revenues are forced to bear these fixed costs over a smaller revenue base compared to larger companies.[46]

However, the auditor attestation is one element of the total audit fees. To gauge the amount spent on the auditor attestation, we asked respondents to our survey to provide us with the amount of total audit fees and the approximate amount attributable to complying with the auditor attestation requirement. Based on our survey results, we estimate that all companies with a market capitalization of less than $10 billion that obtained an auditor attestation in 2012 spent, on average, about $350,000 for auditor attestation fees, representing about 29 percent of their average total audit fees.[47]

Although these costs remain significant for many companies, the cost of implementing the auditor attestation provision has been declining and varies by company size. For example, SEC's 2009 study on internal control over financial reporting found that, among other things, the mean auditor attestation costs declined from about $821,000 to about $584,000 (approximately 29 percent) pre- and –post 2007 reforms for all companies that obtained an auditor attestation. Median costs declined from about $358,000 to $275,000 (approximately 23 percent) pre- and –post 2007

---

[45]GAO, *Sarbanes-Oxley Act: Consideration of Key Principles Needed in Addressing Implementation for Smaller Public Companies*, GAO-06-361 (Washington, D.C.: Apr. 13, 2006).

[46]J. L. Orcutt, "The Case Against Exempting Smaller Reporting Companies from Sarbanes-Oxley Section 404: Why Market-Based Solutions are Not Likely to Harm Ordinary Investors," *Fordham Journal of Corporate & Financial Law*, vol. 14, no. 2 (2009).

[47]The weighted estimates have margins of error of about plus or minus $71,000 and plus or minus 6 percentage points, respectively. In addition to sampling error, the weighted estimates are subject to nonsampling error in that respondents were asked to provide the approximate amount attributable to the auditor attestation requirement. See appendix I for more details.

reforms.[48] According to the study and an academic we interviewed, costs have been declining for a variety of reasons, including companies and auditors gaining experience in the auditor attestation environment and the 2007 SEC and PCAOB guidance. The academic further stated that in the early years of implementation of Section 404(b), initial costs were high for all companies, in part, because they had not previously implemented effective internal controls.[49]

Companies and Others Also Identified Perceived Benefits of Compliance

There are two types of potential benefits or positive impacts—direct and indirect—that companies can receive from complying with the auditor attestation requirement according to one study.[50] Direct benefits are those directly related to improvements in the company's financial reporting process, such as the quality of the internal control structure, the audit committee's confidence in the internal control structure, the quality of financial reporting, and the company's ability to prevent and detect fraud. Indirect benefits are other dimensions that may be affected by changes in the quality of the financial reporting process, such as a company's ability to raise capital, the liquidity of the common stock, and the confidence investors and other users of financial statements may have in the company.

---

[48]Securities and Exchange Commission, *Study of the Sarbanes-Oxley Act of 2002 Section 404 Internal Control over Financial Reporting Requirements* (Washington, D.C.: September 2009).

[49]Internal control is not a new requirement for public companies. In December 1977, as a result of corporate falsification of records and improper accounting, Congress enacted the Foreign Corrupt Practices Act (FCPA). Pub. L. No. 95-213, 91 Stat. 1494 (1977) (codified at 15 U.S.C. §§ 78dd-1-78dd-3). The FCPA's internal accounting control requirements were intended to prevent fraudulent financial reporting, among other things. The FCPA amended the Securities Exchange Act of 1934, Pub. L. No. 73-291, 48 Stat. 881 (codified as amended at 15 U.S.C. §§ 78a-78pp (2012), to require public companies to (1) make and keep books, records, and accounts that in reasonable detail accurately and fairly reflect the transactions and dispositions of assets and (2) develop and maintain a system of internal accounting controls sufficient to provide reasonable assurance that transactions are executed with management authorization and that transactions are recorded in a manner to (a) allow the preparation of financial statements in accordance with generally accepted accounting principles or other applicable criteria and (b) maintain accountability for assets. *Id.* (amending Sec. 13(b) of the Securities Exchange Act of 1934; codified at 15 U.S.C. § 78q(b)).

[50]C. R. Alexander, S. W. Bauguess, G. Bernile, Y. A. Lee, and J. Marietta-Westberg, "The Economic Effects of SOX Section 404 Compliance: A Corporate Insider Perspective," Working paper, (March 2010).

Respondents to our survey identified a number of benefits or positive impacts stemming from compliance with the auditor attestation requirement, although fewer of them perceived indirect benefits compared to direct benefits. Many survey respondents noted that they experienced a number of direct benefits. For example, we estimate that:

- 80 percent of all companies view the quality of their company's internal control structure as benefiting from the auditor attestation;

- 73 percent view their audit committee's confidence in internal control over financial reporting as benefiting from the auditor attestation;

- 53 percent view their financial reporting as benefiting from the requirement; and

- 46 percent view their ability to prevent and detect fraud as benefiting from the auditor attestation (see table 6).

Our findings are consistent with other surveys. In particular, Protiviti's 2013 survey found that, among other things, 80 percent of respondents reported that their company's internal control over financial reporting structure had improved since they began complying with the auditor attestation requirement.[51] However, we also found that, except for improved confidence in the financial reports of other Section 404(b) compliant companies, fewer companies' perceived indirect benefits of the requirement. Specifically, based on our survey results, no more than 30 percent of all companies with less than $10 billion in market capitalization perceived any of the identified indirect benefits (see table 6) as stemming from the auditor attestation requirement.

---

[51]Protiviti, *2013 Sarbanes-Oxley Compliance Survey: Building Value in Your SOX Compliance Program.* 2013.

Table 6: Estimated Percentage of Companies with Market Capitalization Less Than $10 Billion That Perceive Benefits from the Auditor Attestation, by Type of Benefit

Type of benefit	Percentage
Direct benefits:	
Quality of company's internal control structure	80%
Audit committee's confidence in company's internal control over financial reporting	73
Quality of company's financial reporting	53
Ability to prevent and detect fraud	46
Indirect benefits:	
Company's ability to raise capital	16
Investor confidence in company	30
Efficiency of company's operation	19
Efficiency of company's financial reporting process	19
Liquicity of company's common stock	7
Timel ness of company's financial statement audit	11
Company's overall value	16
Confidence in the financial reports of other 404(b) compliant companies	52

Source: GAO survey.

Note: The percentage estimates have a margin of error of plus or minus 15 percentage points or fewer.

A 2013 study conducted by one academic we interviewed examined the earnings quality—how well earnings reflect actual firm performance—of exempt companies and nonexempt companies.[52] The study found a significant deterioration in the quality of earnings for exempt companies, but not for nonexempt companies.[53] In addition, SEC in its 2009 study on

---

[52]A. D. Holder, K. E. Karim, and A. Robin, "Was Dodd-Frank Justified in Exempting Small Firms from Section 404b Compliance?" *Accounting Horizons*, vol. 27 no. 1 (March 2013). There is no single definition of the term "earnings quality."

[53]Two other studies looking at the effect of auditor attestation on exempt and small nonexempt companies had similar findings: one found that compliance with auditor attestat on had improved the quality of financial reporting as measured by materially misstated financial statements (see Nagy, "Section 404 Compliance and Financial Reporting Quality," *Accounting Horizons*, vol. 24, no. 3 (2010), while the other found that auditor attestation benefits small companies via higher revenue quality as measured by discretionary (abnormal) revenues (see G. V. Krishnan and W. Yu, "Do Small Firms Benefit from Auditor Attestation of Internal Control Effectiveness?" *Auditing: A Journal of Practice and Theory,* vol. 31 no. 4 (2012)).

auditors' involvement in internal control over financial reporting noted the following benefits: (1) the independent auditor's assessment of the effectiveness of a company's internal controls results in a more disciplined management assessment process; (2) the independent auditor's expertise can provide management with an additional perspective on the quality of the company's internal controls; and (3) the independent audit of a company's internal controls improves the reliability of a company's internal control disclosures and financial reports. According to some academic researchers, obtaining an auditor attestation can also have a positive impact on a company's cost of capital. One academic we interviewed noted that by complying with the auditor attestation requirement small companies incur lower borrowing costs and therefore a lower cost of capital because investors have greater trust in the accuracy of the companies' financial reporting. Another academic we interviewed noted that companies that do not comply with Section 404(b) of the Sarbanes-Oxley Act reduce investors' confidence in the companies and reduce the transparency and reliability of companies' financial filings. As a result, he would expect their cost of capital to increase. In addition, as discussed later in the report, a 2013 study empirically supports the view that companies that voluntarily comply with the auditor attestation have lower cost of capital.[54]

Measuring the Costs and Benefits of the Auditor Attestation Requirement Is Difficult, and Views Differ on Whether Benefits Exceed Costs

Measuring both the costs and benefits of the auditor attestation requirement is difficult. According several studies, direct costs, such as audit fees, are tangible and immediate and therefore are more readily measured. Indirect costs, such as opportunity costs, are more difficult to measure because they are less tangible. In comparison, however, benefits are more difficult to identify, measure, and quantify than costs because they are intangible and may occur over a longer period.[55] Because measuring the costs and benefits of auditor attestation is difficult, comparing costs and benefits is also challenging.

---

[54]C. A. Cassell, L.A. Myers, and J. Zhou, "The Effects of Voluntary Internal Control Audits on the Cost of Capital," Working paper, (Feb. 13, 2013).

[55]Y. Jahmani and W. A. Dowling, "The Impact of Sarbanes-Oxley Act," *Journal of Business & Economics Research*, vol. 6, no. 10 (2008); Coates IV, John C. "The Goals and Promise of the Sarbanes-Oxley Act," *Journal of Economic Perspectives*, vol. 21, no. 1 (2007); and Chief Financial Officers' Council and the President's Council on Integrity and Efficiency. "Estimating the Costs and Benefits of Rendering an Opinion on Internal Control over Financial Reporting."

Our survey results indicate that the views on whether the benefits associated with auditor attestation compliance outweigh the costs are mixed. According to our survey results, we estimate that about 57 percent of all companies with less than $10 billion in market capitalization view the costs as somewhat or greatly outweighing the benefits; 16 percent of the companies view the benefits as somewhat or greatly outweighing costs; 21 percent of the companies view costs and benefits as being about equal; and 6 percent are not sure. Generally, the perceptions were consistent across companies of different sizes.[56] Some of the reasons companies gave for their views include that the costs are particularly onerous for smaller companies, the time and effort devoted to 404 divert resources away from more value-added activities, and that the attestation overemphasizes testing and the number of controls that are necessary. Some of the reasons companies gave to support the view that the benefits outweigh the costs include that the attestation leads to improved internal control over financial reporting process, increases investor confidence in company's financial reports, and makes it easier to detect fraud.

Companies, trade associations, industry experts, and academics we interviewed expressed various views on the cost-benefit ratio of the auditor attestation. Companies generally assess the costs and benefits of auditor attestation as it relates to themselves and not the marketplace. For example, chief financial officers of two exempt companies that previously had obtained auditor attestations stated that the costs of compliance outweighed the benefits because of the money and time that they (and companies in general) spent on obtaining auditor attestation and the lack of benefits gained from such attestation. In addition, a 2010 empirical study looking at companies of comparable size with public float between $50 million and $100 million found that the net effect of auditor attestation (as measured by stock returns) was negative.[57] The reduction in the market value of nonexempt companies suggests that the costs of

---

[56]For exempt companies that voluntarily complied with the auditor attestation requirement, 63 percent view the costs as somewhat or greatly outweighing the benefits; 19 percent view the benefits as somewhat or greatly outweighing costs; 15 percent view costs and benefits as being about equal; and 3 percent are not sure. For nonexempt companies, 57 percent view the costs as somewhat or greatly outweighing the benefits; 15 percent view the benefits as somewhat or greatly outweighing costs; 21 percent view costs and benefits as being about equal; and 7 percent are not sure.

[57]P. Iliev, "The Effect of SOX Section 404: Costs, Earnings Quality, and Stock Prices," *Journal of Finance,* vol. 65, no. 3 (2010).

compliance may outweigh the benefits for small companies. In contrast, trade associations, industry experts, and some academics we interviewed generally view the benefits as outweighing the costs. They stated generally that even though the auditor attestation is costly to obtain, it has led to more reliable financial reporting, greater transparency and investor protections, or improved internal control systems. SEC and PCAOB officials noted that their agencies have not taken an official position regarding whether the benefits of a company obtaining an auditor attestation outweigh the costs.

Other survey results also show mixed views on whether the benefits associated with auditor attestation compliance outweigh the costs. A 2012 survey of financial, compliance, internal audit, and other executives examined issues companies must address related to the Sarbanes-Oxley Act. The survey results show that even though initial costs and efforts to comply with Section 404 were burdensome, many companies (31 percent of respondents) viewed the benefits as outweighing the costs, in part due to improvement in internal controls.[58] Fifty percent of all responding companies viewed the costs as outweighing the benefits to some degree, and 19 percent viewed the costs and benefits as equal. Large companies held a slightly more positive view of the benefits than small companies. Another 2012 annual survey that looked at audit fees found that 51 percent of the companies that complied with the auditor attestation requirement thought that they had better internal controls as a result and that the attestation was worth the expense.[59] Thirty-seven percent of respondents thought they had better internal controls but that this benefit was not worth the expense, and 7 percent thought that the cost of compliance far exceeded any additional improvement to internal controls. In comparison, the 2005 annual survey showed that during the early implementation of Section 404(b) of Sarbanes-Oxley Act, over 90 percent of survey respondents said that the costs outweighed the benefits.[60]

---

[58]Protiviti, *2012 Sarbanes-Oxley Compliance Survey: Where U.S.-Listed Companies Stand – Reviewing Cost, Time, Effort and Process.* 2012.

[59]Financial Executives International and Financial Executives Research Foundation, *2012 Audit Fee Survey* (Morristown, N.J.: 2012). Financial Executives International is a trade group for financial executives.

[60]Financial Executives International and Financial Executives Research Foundation, *Special Survey on Sarbanes-Oxley Section 404 Implementation* (Morristown, N.J.: 2005).

GAO-13-582 Auditor Attestation on Internal Controls

Auditor Attestations Appear to Positively Affect Investor Confidence, and Disclosure of Compliance Status Could Enhance Investor Protection

Research suggests that auditor attestation generally has a positive effect on investor confidence. Although exempt companies are currently not required to disclose whether they voluntarily complied with the auditor attestation requirement in their annual reports, doing so would provide investors with important information that may influence their investment decisions.

Most Empirical Studies We Reviewed Suggest That Auditor Attestation Has a Positive Impact on Investor Confidence

Recent empirical studies we reviewed found that auditor attestation of internal controls generally has a positive impact on investor confidence. Investor confidence is considered an indirect benefit to companies that comply with the auditor attestation requirement. Specifically, an auditor attestation of internal controls helps to reduce information asymmetries between a company's management and investors.[61] With increased transparency and better financial reporting due to reliable third-party attestation, investors face a lower risk of losses from fraud. This lowered risk has a number of positive consequences for companies, such as enabling them to pay less for the capital as more confident investors require a lower rate of return on their money.

Because investor confidence is difficult to measure directly, empirical research has examined the impact of auditor attestation on other variables that are considered proxies for investor confidence, including the cost of equity and debt capital, stock performance, and liquidity.[62] As

---

[61]Information asymmetry refers to the fact that managers of a company typically know more than outsiders about the conditions of the company and its future prospects. They can exploit this information asymmetry to help the company or themselves by, for example, releasing limited or biased information. These actions would affect the ability of investors to make good investment decisions and in turn lead to inefficiencies, such as misallocation of capital.

[62]Our focus in this section is on recent empirical research about the impact on investor confidence of auditor attestations required by the Sarbanes-Oxley Act's Section 404(b). There is a large body of empirical research that has investigated different aspects of the implementation of the Sarbanes-Oxley Act's Sections 302, 404(a), and 404(b) since the passage of the act. See A. Schneider, A. Gramling, D. R. Hermanson and Z. Ye, "A Review of Academic Literature on Internal Control Reporting Under SOX," *Journal of Accounting Literature*, vol. 28 (2009).

described below, such research has found that the auditor attestation increases investor confidence.

- A 2012 study examined exempt and nonexempt companies with market capitalization between $25 million and $125 million. This study found that the market value of equity—as measured by the common stock price—is positively associated with the book value of equity—which is an element in financial statements—but that this relationship is stronger for nonexempt companies.[63] In other words, investors appear to put greater trust on the book value of equity of companies that are subject to auditor attestation compared to those companies that are not. As a result, book value is more likely to have a positive effect on market value if the auditor attestation is present. These results are consistent with the notion that the auditor attestation provides useful and relevant information to investors.

- A 2013 study found that exempt companies that voluntarily comply with the auditor attestation enjoy a lower cost of capital. Specifically, both the cost of equity and the cost of debt are significantly lower for companies that voluntarily comply with the requirement compared to those exempt companies that do not.[64] These results are consistent with the view that auditor attestation leads to higher investor confidence and that voluntary compliance with the requirement reduces the risk companies present to investors. This lowered risk, in turn, reduces the risk premium that investors demand to hold these companies' stocks or bonds.

- A 2012 study examined the equity market response to the 2009 proposed permanent exemption from the auditor attestation requirement for public companies with a public float of less than

---

[63]G. V. Krishnan and W. Yu, "Do Small Firms Benefit from Auditor Attestation of Internal Control Effectiveness?" *Auditing: A Journal of Practice and Theory,* vol. 34, no.1 (2012).

[64]C. A. Cassell, L.A. Myers, and J. Zhou, "The Effects of Voluntary Internal Control Audits on the Cost of Capital," Working paper, (Feb. 13, 2013).

75 million.[65] The study found a negative market response to the exemption but less so for those companies that voluntarily complied before 2009. It also found that to reduce information asymmetry, companies that voluntarily comply use their compliance as a signal to the marketplace of the superior quality of their financial reporting—a signal that is credible because it is costly and difficult to imitate by companies with weak internal controls.[66] Also, companies that voluntarily complied with auditor attestation had significant increases in liquidity.[67]

Other research supports the view that auditor attestation of internal control effectiveness matters for investors and other market participants insofar as adverse auditor reports have negative consequences for companies. Such consequences include higher cost of debt (and possibly

---

[65]More specifically, the study undertakes an empirical investigation of the response to the November 2009 Garrett-Adler amendment approved by the House Financial Services Committee, which proposed to exempt smaller public companies from the auditor attestation requirement. (*see* Investor Protection Act of 2009, H.R. 3817, 111th Cong. § 606). K. Brown, P. Pacharn, J. Li, E. Mohammad, F. A. Elayan, and F. Chu, "The Valuation Effect and Motivations of Voluntary Compliance with Auditor's Attestation under Sarbanes-Oxley Act Section 404 (B)," Working paper, (Jan. 15, 2012).

[66]Signaling may provide a benefit especially to small, high-growth companies that need capital to expand. Exempt companies have to balance the potential benefits and cost of voluntary compliance, as auditors' involvement increases the likelihood that internal control deficiencies will be discovered and disclosed, with negative consequences.

[67]This increase suggests that auditor attestation enhances public confidence in financial reports leading to a flight to quality by investors and an increase in liquidity, in which investors move their capital away from assets perceived as risky in favor of those viewed as safe.

higher cost of equity), lower probability that lenders will extend lines of credit, stricter loan terms, and unfavorable stock recommendations.[68]

While most research findings we reviewed suggest auditor attestation provides valuable information to investors and has a positive effect on confidence, a 2011 study questions the value of the auditor attestation for small companies.[69] Looking at exempt and small nonexempt companies with market capitalization of $300 million or less, the study finds that small companies that became nonexempt, and therefore subject to the auditor attestation requirement, in 2004 experienced a statistically significant increase in their material weakness disclosure rate, but companies that remained exempt saw similar increases through their management reports under Section 404(a) of the Sarbanes-Oxley Act. The results suggest that auditor attestation provides little additional information to investors in terms of detecting material weaknesses because there is no statistically significant difference in the rate of disclosure of material weakness between the two types of companies.

Anecdotal Information Also Suggests Auditor Attestation Can Positively Impact Investor Confidence

The majority of academics and market participants we interviewed suggest that having auditor attestation positively impacts investor confidence. Specifically, they told us that the involvement of auditors in attesting to the effectiveness of internal controls improves the reliability of the financial reporting and serves to protect investors. As a result, they said, the exemption granted to small companies is likely to reduce investor confidence because these companies already have greater

---

[68]See for example, A. Crabtree and J. J. Maher, "Credit Ratings, Cost of Debt, and Internal Control Disclosures: A Comparison of SOC 302 and SOX 404," *The Journal of Applied Business Research,* vol. 28, no. 5, (2012); J.B. Kim, B.Y. Song, L. Zhang, "Internal Control Weakness and Bank Loan Contracting: Evidence from SOX Section 404 Disclosures," *The Accounting Review,* vol. 86, no. 4 (2011); D. Dhaliwal, C. Hogan, R. Trezevant, and M. Wilkins, "Internal Control Disclosures, Monitoring, and the Cost of Debt," *The Accounting Review,* vol. 86, no. 4 (2011); H. Ashbaugh-Skaife, D. Collins, W. Kinney, and R. LaFond, "The Effect of SOX Internal Control Deficiencies on Firm Risk and Cost of Equity," *Journal of Accounting Research,* vol. 47, no. 1 (2009); A. Schneider and B.K. Church, "The Effect of Auditors' Internal Control Opinions on Loan Decisions," *Journal of Accounting and Public Policy,* vol. 27, no.1 (2008); S. K. Asare and A. Wright, "The Effect of Type of Internal Control Report on Users' Confidence in the Accompanying Financial Statement Audit Report," *Contemporary Accounting Research,* vol. 29, no. 1 (2012).

[69]W. R. Kinney and M. L. Shepardson, "Do Control Effectiveness Disclosures Require SOX 404(b) Internal Control Audits? A Natural Experiment with Small U.S. Public Companies," *Journal of Accounting Research,* vol. 49, no. 2. (2011).

informational asymmetry. They said that according to academic and other studies, small companies are also more likely than large ones to have serious internal control problems. Furthermore, they commented that management's report on internal controls alone is often uninformative because management often fails to detect internal control deficiencies or classifies them as less severe than they are. Some market participants also told us that any company accessing capital markets, regardless of size, should be required to comply with the auditor attestation requirement as investors in any company, large or small, are entitled to the same investor protection.

Our survey results also indicate that some companies view auditor attestation as contributing to investor confidence, which is similar to findings from others' studies and surveys. Our survey results show that the majority of respondents are more confident in the financial reports of companies that comply with the auditor attestation requirement than companies that do not. In addition, we estimate that 30 percent of responding nonexempt and exempt companies that voluntarily comply thought that the requirement increased investor confidence in their own company, while 20 percent were not sure and the remaining 50 percent reported no impact. This perspective is consistent with the results from an in-depth 2009 telephone survey SEC conducted of a small group of financial statement users—such as lenders, securities analysts, credit rating agencies, and other investors—regarding their views on the benefits of auditor attestation. These SEC survey respondents indicated that the auditor's attestation report provides additional benefits to users and other investors beyond the management's report under Section 404(a) and that the requirement generally has a positive impact on their confidence in companies' financial reports. Moreover, in response to a 2010 Center for Audit Quality (CAQ) survey of individual investors, almost two-thirds of investors said they were concerned about exempting companies with annual revenues of under $75 million from the independent auditor attestation requirement, suggesting that the requirement has a positive effect on individual investors' confidence in the financial information generated by smaller companies.[70] Similarly, in a

---

[70]Center for Audit Quality, *The CAQ's Fourth Annual Individual Investor Survey*, September 2010. The Center for Audit Quality is a nonprofit group whose board includes leaders from the public company auditing firms, the American Institute of CPAs, and three members from outside the public company auditing profession. The organization is affiliated with the American Institute of CPAs and seeks to enhance investor confidence and public trust in the global capital markets.

2012 survey of investors conducted by the PCAOB Investor Advisory Group on the role, relevance, and value of the audit, over 60 percent of respondents said that the auditor's opinion on the effectiveness of internal controls is critical in making investment decisions.[71] Further, in a 2012 survey of individual investors by CAQ, 70 percent of the respondents identified independent audits in general as the most effective means of protecting their interests.[72]

Disclosure of Auditor Attestation Status Could Enhance Transparency

Explicit disclosure of auditor attestation status in exempt companies' annual reports could quickly provide investors useful information that may influence their investment decisions. Currently, exempt companies are not required to disclose in their annual reports whether they have voluntarily obtained an auditor attestation on their internal controls. From 2005 through 2010, SEC granted small public companies multiple extensions from having to comply with the auditor attestation requirement. During this time of forbearance, SEC required exempt companies to include a general statement in their annual report that the company was not required to comply with the auditor attestation requirement because of SEC's grant of temporary exemption status. According to SEC officials, the statement served to provide investors who may have been looking for the attestation an explanation of its absence. SEC granted its final temporary exemption to take effect on June 15, 2010, prior to the passage of the Dodd-Frank Act. SEC did not require exempt companies to include the disclosure statement when implementing the provision of the Dodd-Frank Act that created the permanent exemption.

SEC officials said that it is not common for the agency to require a company to disclose compliance status for requirements that are not applicable to the company—which, according to SEC officials, could potentially influence a company's behavior. Further, SEC officials noted that information on the company's filing status—and, therefore exemption status—can be found in the company's annual reports and other

[71]In addition, about 47 percent of respondents reported using the auditor's report "always" or "often" when making investment decisions, with about 27 percent reporting using it "sometimes." PCAOB Investor Advisory Group, March 28, 2012, presentation on the Role, Relevance, and Value of the Audit.

[72]Center for Audit Quality, *The CAQ's Sixth Annual Main Street Investor Survey*, September 2012.

documents, which are available to all investors.[73] Therefore, SEC officials stated that such information allows investors to determine whether an attestation has been obtained. However, while this information is available, a company's attestation status is not readily apparent without some knowledge or interpretation of the current reporting requirements. As noted earlier, SEC has previously required companies to provide additional clarity on their compliance with the auditor attestation requirement. Thus, requiring companies to explicitly disclose their auditor attestation status would be consistent with its past action.

Further, federal securities laws require public companies to disclose relevant information to investors to aid them in their investment decisions.[74] Many market participants we interviewed consider the external auditor's assessment of the effectiveness of a company's internal control over financial reporting to be important information for investors. Thus, many market participants we interviewed and companies we surveyed noted that exempt companies should be required to explicitly disclose whether or not they obtained an auditor attestation to make the information more transparent for investors. In particular, according to the results of our survey, we estimate that 57 percent of all companies with less than $10 billion in market capitalization are in favor of requiring exempt companies to disclose whether they have voluntarily obtained an auditor attestation. A representative from one company said "I believe there is an assumption that SEC-listed companies are in compliance with 404. If companies are not, they should disclose such." A representative from another company said that "If investors value the independent audit, then they should be made aware of situations where such audit has not been performed. Investors should not have to interpret the regulations to know if the audit is required." Some companies we surveyed that were not in favor of such disclosure generally believed that investors can get the information from the audit opinion in the annual report. As of year-end 2011, approximately 300 exempt companies had voluntarily complied with the auditor attestation requirement. Although information on voluntary compliance with the auditor attestation requirement is determinable, having the information explicitly disclosed could benefit investors. Such

[73]See for example, Items 8 and 9A in the annual reports filed with SEC and Item 308(a)(4) of Regulation S-K, as amended in 2010.

[74]See generally Securities Act of 1933, §§ 7, 8, 11, 12, and 17; Securities Exchange Act of 1934, §§ 10, 13, and 14.

disclosure would increase transparency and investor protection by making investors more aware of this important investment information.

Conclusions

Investors need accurate financial information with which to make informed investment decisions, and effective internal controls are necessary for accurate and reliable financial reporting. The attestation requirement is part of legislation aimed at helping to protect investors by, among other things, improving the quality of corporate financial reporting and disclosures. Perceptions of the costs and benefits of auditor attestation continue to vary among companies and others, but among other benefits, obtaining auditor attestation appears to have a positive impact on investor confidence. In addition, our analysis found that companies (both exempt and nonexempt) that obtained an auditor attestation generally had fewer financial restatements than those that did not, which suggests that knowing whether a company has obtained the auditor attestation may be useful for investors in gauging the reliability of a company's financial reporting. However, because SEC regulations currently do not require explicit statements regarding the voluntary attainment of auditor attestation, investors may have to interpret reporting requirements and filings to determine whether exempt companies have obtained an auditor attestation. Previously, when certain companies were temporarily exempt from the auditor attestation requirement, SEC required explicit disclosure of exemption status in companies' annual reports. However, SEC eliminated this requirement in 2010 when companies of certain sizes were permanently exempted. Federal securities laws require public companies to disclose relevant information to investors to aid them in their investment decisions. Although information on a company's exempt status is available to investors, explicit disclosure would increase transparency and investor protection by making investors readily aware of whether a company has obtained an auditor attestation on internal controls. The disclosure could serve as an important indicator of the reliability of a company's financial reporting, which may influence investors' decisions.

Recommendation for Executive Action

To enhance transparency and investor protection, we recommend that SEC consider requiring public companies, where applicable, to explicitly disclose whether they obtained an auditor attestation of their internal controls.

Agency and Third-Party Comments and Our Evaluation

We provided a draft of the report to the SEC Chairman for her review and comment. SEC provided written comments that are summarized below and reprinted in appendix II. We also provided a draft of the report to PCAOB and relevant excerpts of the draft report to Audit Analytics for technical review. We received technical comments from SEC, PCAOB, and Audit Analytics that were incorporated as appropriate.

In its written comments, SEC did not comment on our recommendation that it consider requiring public companies to explicitly disclose whether they have obtained an internal control attestation. Rather, SEC confirmed, as described in the draft report, that a nonaccelerated filer (referred to as an exempt company in our report) does not have to explicitly disclose whether it obtained an auditor attestation report on its internal controls in its annual report. However, SEC stated that this fact can be easily determined by investors from information that is already disclosed in the annual report. In addition, SEC stated that investors can also find information regarding the existence of an opinion on internal controls by looking at the audit report in the company's filing. SEC also noted that PCAOB standards permit an auditor that is not engaged to opine on internal controls to include a statement in its report on the financial statements indicating that it is not opining on the internal controls. In our report, we acknowledge that information needed to determine a company's auditor attestation status is available. However, because an explicit statement on the company's status is not required, investors must deduce the company's status from the available information. Explicit disclosure could significantly decrease the potential for investors to misinterpret the information regarding a company's audit attestation status. Such disclosure would increase transparency and investor protection by making investors readily aware of this important investment information. We therefore maintain that the disclosure warrants further consideration by SEC.

We are sending copies of this report to appropriate congressional committees, SEC, PCAOB, Audit Analytics and other interested parties. In addition, the report is available at no charge on the GAO website at http://www.gao.gov.

If you or your staff have any questions about this report, please contact me at (202) 512-8678 or clowersa@gao.gov. Contact points for our Offices of Congressional Relations and Public Affairs may be found on the last page of this report. GAO staff who made key contributions to this report are listed in appendix IV.

A. Nicole Clowers
Director
Financial Markets and
Community Investment

Appendix I: Objectives, Scope, and Methodology

This report discusses: (1) how the number of financial statement restatements compares between exempt and nonexempt companies; (2) the costs and benefits for nonexempt companies as well as exempt companies that voluntarily comply with the auditor attestation requirement; and (3) what is known about the extent to which investor confidence in the integrity of financial statements is affected by whether or not companies comply with the auditor attestation requirement. We define exempt companies as those with less than $75 million in public float (nonaccelerated filers) and nonexempt companies as those with $75 million or more in public float (accelerated filers). For the purposes of this report, we define exempt companies as those with less than $75 million in public float (nonaccelerated filers) and nonexempt companies as those with $75 million or more in public float (accelerated filers).

To address all three objectives, we reviewed and analyzed information from a variety of sources, including the Sarbanes-Oxley Act of 2002 (Sarbanes-Oxley Act), the Dodd-Frank Wall Street Reform and Consumer Protection Act (Dodd-Frank Act), relevant regulatory press releases and related public comment letters, and available research studies.[1] We also interviewed officials from the Securities and Exchange Commission (SEC) and the Public Company Accounting Oversight Board (PCAOB), and we interviewed chief financial officers of small public companies, representatives of relevant trade associations (representing individual and institutional investors, accounting companies, financial analysts and investment professionals, and financial executives), a large pension fund, a credit rating agency, academics knowledgeable about accounting issues, and industry experts.

Comparison of Exempt and Nonexempt Financial Restatements

To determine the number of financial statement restatements (referred to as financial restatements) and trends, we analyzed data from the Audit Analytics database from 2005 through 2011.[2] We used the Audit Analytics' Auditor Opinion database to generate the population of exempt

---

[1]Pub. L. No. 107-204, 116 Stat. 745 (2002); Pub. L. No. 111-203, 124 Stat. 1376 (2010).

[2]Audit Analytics is an online market intelligence service that provides information on SEC registrants. Audit Analytics maintains a proprietary database containing information from the filings public companies submit to SEC, such as audit fees, audit opinions, and financial restatements.

and nonexempt companies in each year from 2005 through 2011.[3] Our
analysis does not include 2012 data because 2012 small-company data
was incomplete. According to Audit Analytics, the incomplete data was
often due to the fact that small companies had not yet filed the relevant
information with SEC. The sample we used to produce the population of
exempt and nonexempt companies does not include subsidiaries of a
public company, registered investment companies, or asset-backed
securities issuers. Once we excluded these companies from the entire
population, we grouped the remaining companies based on their filing
status (i.e., nonaccelerated filer, smaller reporting company, accelerated
filer, large accelerated filer, and filers that did not disclose their filing
status).[4] Exempt companies are nonaccelerated filers, including smaller
reporting companies. For our purposes, we grouped companies that did
not disclose their filing status but whose market capitalization was less
than $75 million with exempt companies.[5] We also identified for each year
from 2005 through 2011 exempt companies that voluntarily complied with
the integrated audit requirement as indicated in the data. Nonexempt
companies are accelerated filers and large accelerated filers. For our
purposes, we grouped companies that did not disclose their filing status
but whose market capitalization was equal to or greater than $75 million
with nonexempt companies. We excluded companies that did not disclose
their filing status and did not have a reported market capitalization.

We then used Audit Analytics' Restatement database, which contains
company information (e.g., assets, revenues, restatements, market
capitalization, location, and industry classification code) to identify the

---

[3]The Audit Opinion data set covers all SEC registrants who have disclosed their auditor's
report on the audit of the financial statements in electronic filings and represents the data
concerning the auditor's opinion.

[4]The designation of "Large Accelerated Filer" was not approved by SEC until December
2005, and the designation of "Smaller Reporting Company" was not approved by SEC
until January 2008. See Revisions to Accelerated Filer Definition and Accelerated
Deadlines for Filing Periodic Reports, 70 Fed. Reg. 76626 (Dec. 27, 2005); Smaller
Reporting Company Regulatory Relief and Simplification, 73 Fed. Reg. 934 (Jan. 4, 2008).

[5]Companies that did not disclose their filing status include Canadian Form 40-F filers and
others. We used market capitalization because Audit Analytics database does not capture
companies' public float. Market capitalization is defined as the total dollar market value of
all of a company's outstanding shares and is calculated by multiplying the number of a
company's outstanding shares by the current market price of one share. Public float is a
subset of market capitalization. SEC defines public float as the worldwide aggregate
market value of voting and nonvoting common equity held by nonaffiliates of the filer. See
12 C.F.R. § 240.12b-2.

number of financial restatements from 2005 through 2011 based on our
population of exempt companies, exempt companies that voluntarily
complied, and nonexempt companies. Using this database, we identified
6,436 financial restatements by 4,536 public companies, 2,834 of which
were exempt companies. We used Audit Analytics' 69 classifications to
classify the type of financial restatements into six categories: core
expenses (i.e., ongoing operating expenses), noncore expenses (i.e.,
nonoperating or nonrecurring expenses), revenue recognition (i.e.,
improperly record revenues), reclassifications and disclosures, underlying
events (i.e., accounting for mergers and acquisitions), and other.[6] The
majority of restatements we classified were the result of an accounting
rule misapplication.[7] To identify audit costs of compliance, we analyzed
data from Audit Analytics' Auditor Opinion database, which contains
auditors' report information such as audit fees, nonaudit fees, auditor
name, audit opinions, revenues, and company size, among other
information from 2005 through 2011. Our analyses of audit costs do not
include 2012 data because 2012 small-company data was incomplete.
The incomplete data was often due to the fact that small companies had
not yet filed the relevant information with SEC. We tested a sample of the
Audit Analytics database information and found it to be reliable for our
purposes. For example, we cross-checked random samples from each of
Audit Analytics' databases with information on financial restatements,
filing status, and internal controls from SEC's Electronic Data Gathering,
Analysis, and Retrieval system. We also spoke with other users of Audit
Analytics data as well as Audit Analytics officials. In addition, we reviewed
relevant research studies and papers on the impact of compliance with
the internal control audits on financial restatements. We consider the
information to be reliable for our purpose of determining financial
statement restatement trends and audit fee calculations.

---

[6]Five of the six categories are based on the classification scheme developed by
academics Zoe-Vonna Palmrose and Susan Scholz. The "other" category was developed
by GAO and comprises financial restatements that were not included in one of the other
categories.

[7]The Audit Analytics Restatement database uses a taxonomy to group restatements into
three categories (1) restatements based on accounting rule misapplication failure (i.e.,
generally accepted accounting principles); (2) restatements based on financial fraud,
irregularities, and misrepresentations; and (3) restatements based on accounting and
clerical errors. The database includes a fourth category to identify significant additional
issues in the restatement (i.e., material weakness or loan covenant violation).

Costs and Benefits of Auditor Attestation Compliance

To examine the characteristics of publicly traded companies that complied, either voluntarily or because required, with the requirement to obtain an independent auditor attestation of their internal controls, we conducted a web-based survey of companies that had either voluntarily complied or were required to comply with the integrated audit requirement in any year between 2004 and 2011. Based on a list of publicly traded companies obtained from Audit Analytics, we identified 4,053 companies that had either voluntarily complied with the integrated audit requirement in any year from 2004 through 2011 or that were required to comply in 2011 as determined by their filing status.[8] We stratified the population into three strata by first identifying the nonaccelerated voluntary filers. These are companies that voluntarily complied with the integrated audit requirement in any year from 2004 through 2011. Since our primary focus was on the nonaccelerated voluntary filers, we selected all 392 of these companies.[9] From the remaining companies in the population, we created two additional strata based on 2011 filing status, and we took a random sample of companies from the remaining strata. The sample sizes for the remaining strata were determined to produce a proportion estimate within each stratum that would achieve a precision of plus or minus 10 percentage points or less, at the 95 percent confidence level. Finally, we increased the sample size based on the expected response rate of 40 percent. We submitted our survey to a total of 850 companies from the original population of 4,053.

We identified 104 companies in our sample that were closed, merged with another company, or improperly included in the sampling frame. We received valid responses from 195 out of the remaining 746 sampled companies (see table 7). The weighted response rate, which accounts for the differential sampling fractions within strata, is 25 percent.

[8]In this report, we use Audit Analytics data, which are based on public filings made with SEC, to develop the population for our survey. SEC uses public float to determine companies' filing status as of the companies' most recently completed second fiscal quarter. To account for changes that could occur with regard to the companies' filing status as of their recently completed second fiscal quarter and the end of the year, we filtered the populations by market capitalization because public float data were not available in the Audit Analytics database.

[9]This figure was based on the unique number of exempt firms who voluntarily complied with the requirement from 2004 through 2011 based on their filing status and market capitalization rate greater than zero and less than $75 million.

Table 7: Survey Sample Disposition

Stratum	Population size	Sample size	Out of scope	Respondents
1. Nonaccelerated voluntary filers	392	392	92	93
2. Accelerated filers	1,620	228	9	56
3. Large accelerated filers	2,041	230	3	46
Total	**4,053**	**850**	**104**	**195**

Source: GAO.

We conducted this survey in a web-based format. The questionnaire was designed by a GAO survey specialist in collaboration with GAO staff with subject-matter expertise. The questionnaire was also reviewed by experts at SEC. We pretested drafts of our questionnaire with three public companies of different sizes to ensure that the questions and response categories were clear, that terminology was used correctly, and that the questions did not place an undue burden on the respondents. The pretests were conducted by telephone with company financial executives in Iowa, Virginia, and Washington, D.C. Pretests included GAO methodologists and GAO subject-matter experts. Based on the feedback received from the pretests, we made changes to the content and format of some survey questions. We directed our survey to the chief executive officer, chief financial officer, or chief accounting officer, whose names and email addresses we obtained from Nexis. We activated our web-based survey on December 17, 2012, and closed the survey on February 19, 2013. We sent follow-up emails on three occasions to remind respondents to complete the survey and conducted telephone follow-ups to increase the response rate.

Because our survey was based on a random sample of the population, it is subject to sampling errors. In addition, the practical difficulties of conducting any survey may introduce nonsampling errors. For example, difference in how a particular question is interpreted or the sources of information available to respondents may introduce errors. We took steps, such as those described above, to minimize such nonsampling errors in the development of the questionnaire and the data collection and data analysis stages as well. For example, because this was a web-based survey, respondents entered their responses directly into the database, reducing the possibility of data-entry error. Finally, when the data were analyzed, a second independent analyst reviewed all computer programs. We conducted an analysis of our survey results to identify potential sources of nonresponse bias using two methods. First, we examined the

response propensity of the sampled companies by several demographic
characteristics. These characteristics included market capitalization size
categories, region, and sector. Our second method consisted of
comparing weighted estimates from respondents and nonrespondents to
known population values for total market capitalization. We conducted
statistical tests of differences, at the 95 percent confidence level, between
estimates and known population values, and between respondents and
nonrespondents. We determined that there was significant bias induced
by the largest companies (measured by market capitalization) not
responding to the survey. In other words, we found that companies with
market capitalization over $10 billion were underrepresented in our
sample. However, we found no evidence of substantial nonresponse bias
based on these characteristics when generalizing to the population of
companies with market capitalization less than or equal to $10 billion.
Therefore, we adjusted the scope of our survey to include only those
companies with market capitalization of less than or equal to $10 billion
(see table 8).

Table 8: Sample Disposition for Adjusted Target Population

Stratum	Population size	Sample size	Out of scope	Respondents
1. Nonaccelerated voluntary filers	392	392	92	93
2. Accelerated filers	1,620	228	9	56
3. Large accelerated filers	1,585	176	1	43
Total	**3,597**	**796**	**102**	**192**

Source: GAO.

Because we found no evidence of substantial nonresponse bias when
generalizing to the adjusted target population and the weighted response
rate of 25 percent, we determined that weighted estimates generated
from these survey results are generalizable to the population of in-scope
companies.[10] We generated weighted estimates and generalized the

---

[10]In-scope population refers to the population to which we are generalizing that includes
all publically traded companies with a public float value of less than $75 million that
voluntarily complied with the integrated audit requirement in any year from 2004 through
2011 as well as those public companies with a market capitalization under $10 billion that
were required to comply in 2011 and that remained in business at the time of the survey.

results to the estimated in-scope population of 3,432 companies (plus or
minus 42 companies).[11]

Because we followed a probability procedure based on random
selections, our sample is only one of a large number of samples that we
might have drawn. Since each sample could have provided different
estimates, we express our confidence in the precision of our particular
sample's results as a 95 percent confidence interval. This is the interval
that would contain the actual population value for 95 percent of the
samples we could have drawn. As a result, we are 95 percent confident
that each of the confidence intervals in this report includes the true values
in the study population. All percentage estimates presented in this report
have a margin of error of plus or minus 15 percentage points or fewer,
and all estimates of averages have a relative margin of error of plus or
minus 20 percent or less, unless otherwise noted.

To obtain information on the impact of obtaining an auditor attestation on
a company's cost of capital, we included questions in our web-based
survey to large and small public companies of various industries about
this matter, interviewed trade associations, industry experts, a large
pension fund, and academics; and reviewed relevant academic and SEC
research studies.

Investor Confidence and Integrity of Financial Statements

To examine the extent to which investor confidence in the integrity of
financial statements is affected by companies' compliance with the
auditor attestation requirement, we reviewed relevant empirical literature
written by academic researchers, as well as recent surveys, studies,
reports, and articles by others. To identify these studies, we asked for
recommendations from academics, SEC, PCAOB, and representatives of
organizations that address issues related to the auditor attestation
requirement. We reviewed bibliographies of papers we obtained to
identify additional material. In addition, we conducted searches of online
databases such as ProQuest and Nexis using keywords to link Section
404(b) of the Sarbanes-Oxley Act with investor confidence. We also
conducted interviews with agencies and organizations, as well as

---

[11]Since we were able to identify 104 out of scope companies in our sample, we can
logically expect that there are out of scope companies in the population that were not
sampled. The 3,423 represents an estimated number of in-scope companies and because
it is based on a random sample, we can compute a margin of error of plus or minus 42
companies around that estimate.

academics and other knowledgeable individuals who focus on issues related to investor confidence and the auditor attestation requirement. Moreover, we interviewed small public companies exempt from auditor attestation but who nonetheless complied with the requirement. In addition, we reviewed surveys undertaken by various government agencies and organizations to gauge the impact of the auditor attestation on investor confidence. We conducted a focused review of the research related to Section 404(b) of the Sarbanes-Oxley Act and summarized the recent studies most relevant to our objective. The empirical research discussed may have limitations, such as accuracy of measures and proxies used. We reviewed published works by academic researchers, government agencies, and organizations with expertise in the field. We performed our searches from September 2012 through May 2013. We assessed the reliability of these studies for use as corroborating evidence and found them to be reliable for our purposes. We also included questions in our web-based survey to large and small public companies of various industries about this matter. Lastly, we reviewed relevant federal securities laws, the Securities Act of 1933 and the Securities Exchange Act of 1934.[12]

We conducted this performance audit from May 2012 to July 2013 in accordance with generally accepted government auditing standards. Those standards require that we plan and perform the audit to obtain sufficient, appropriate evidence to provide a reasonable basis for our findings and conclusions based on our audit objectives. We believe that the evidence obtained provides a reasonable basis for our findings and conclusions based on our audit objectives.

---

[12]Securities Act of 1933, Pub. L. No. 73-22, 48 Stat. 74 (codified as amended at 15 U.S.C. §§ 77a-77aa (2012)); Securities Exchange Act of 1934, Pub. L. No. 73-291, 48 Stat. 881 (codified as amended at 15 U.S.C. §§ 78a-78pp (2012)).

Appendix II: Comments from the Securities and Exchange Commission

UNITED STATES
SECURITIES AND EXCHANGE COMMISSION
WASHINGTON, D.C. 20549

June 20, 2013

A. Nicole Clowers
Director
Financial Markets and Community Investment
U.S. Government Accountability Office
441 G Street, NW
Washington, DC 20548

Dear Ms. Clowers:

Thank you for the opportunity to review the draft report required by Section 989I of the Dodd-Frank Wall Street Reform and Consumer Protection Act. We greatly appreciate the valuable insight that the Government Accountability Office ("GAO") has provided regarding the importance of reliable financial reporting, including the importance of internal control over financial reporting ("ICFR") and the independent audit function.

The draft report correctly identifies that a non-accelerated filer that does not voluntarily include in its annual report an attestation report from its auditor on ICFR is not required to disclose this fact explicitly. We believe that this fact can be easily determined by investors from information that is already disclosed in the annual report. An issuer is required to indicate its filing status on the cover page of its annual report, clearly disclosing whether the issuer is a non-accelerated filer and, therefore, exempt from the auditor attestation requirement. Further, SEC rules require any issuer that includes an auditor's attestation report on ICFR in its annual report, whether the attestation report is voluntary or required, to include a statement that the attestation report is included in the annual report.[1] As a result, non-accelerated filers that voluntarily provide an attestation report are readily identified.

In addition, investors can also find information regarding the existence of an opinion on ICFR by looking at the audit report in the issuer's filing. For example, when the auditor is engaged to opine on ICFR, Public Company Accounting Oversight Board ("PCAOB") standards permit the auditor to issue a combined report, which would contain both an opinion on the financial statements and an opinion on ICFR.[2] If the auditor chooses to issue a separate attestation report on ICFR, PCAOB standards require an explicit statement that the issuer's ICFR

---

[1] See Item 308(a)(4) of Regulation S-K.

[2] See PCAOB Auditing Standard ("AS") No. 5, paragraph 86.

A. Nicole Clowers
Page 2

has been audited.[3] In the case of either combined or separate reports, the fact that the auditor opined on ICFR is clearly disclosed in the auditor's report on the financial statements.

When the auditor is not engaged to opine on ICFR, PCAOB standards permit the auditor to also include in its report on the financial statements an explicit statement of this fact and that the auditor does not express an opinion on ICFR.[4] The PCAOB has announced that, as part of its standard-setting agenda, it plans to propose changes to the auditor's reporting model later in 2013. As part of this project, we understand that the PCAOB staff intends to recommend that the PCAOB seek specific feedback on requiring, as opposed to permitting, these explicit statements.

We remain dedicated to continuously evaluating and improving our disclosure requirements and to making sure that investors have the information they need to make informed investment decisions. We appreciate GAO's attention to these important issues, and we would like to thank you and your staff for your work.

Sincerely,

Paul Beswick
Chief Accountant
Office of the Chief Accountant

Lona Nallengara
Acting Director
Division of Corporation Finance

---

[3] See PCAOB AS No. 5, paragraph 88.

[4] See PCAOB AU Section 9550.10.

Appendix III: GAO Survey of Accelerated Filers and Nonaccelerated Filers

Survey of Accelerated and Non-accelerated Filers Regarding Section 404(b) of the Sarbanes-Oxley Act

United States Government Accountability Office

Introduction

The U.S. Government Accountability Office (GAO) is the independent evaluation and investigative agency of the Congress. As statutorily mandated by Section 989I of the Dodd-Frank Wall Street Reform and Consumer Protection Act of 2010 (Dodd-Frank Act), GAO is currently conducting a study with respect to the auditor attestation requirement under Section 404(b) of the Sarbanes-Oxley Act of 2002 (Sarbanes-Oxley Act) for securities issuers whose market capitalization is less than $75 million (referred to as non-accelerated filers). Section 989G(a) of the Dodd-Frank Act amended the Sarbanes-Oxley Act to permanently exempt non-accelerated filers from having to comply with the auditor attestation requirement under Section 404(b) of the Sarbanes-Oxley Act.

Your participation in the survey will help us provide a comprehensive report to the Congress. In reporting the results of the survey, we will not tie individual responses to you or your company by name. GAO generally reports the results of surveys in aggregate. While GAO may incorporate individual responses in the report, we will do so in a manner designed to ensure that individual respondents cannot be identified. Further, GAO will not otherwise release individually identifiable versions of responses unless required by law or requested by a member of Congress.

To learn more about completing the survey, printing your responses, and whom to contact if you have questions, click here for help.

Thank you in advance for your cooperation.

Section 1 - Background Information

1. Please provide contact information for the primary person completing this questionnaire in the event we need to contact you to clarify a survey response.

Name:	
Company:	
E-mail address:	
Office telephone:	
Title	[none]
Specify other title:	

> **Please note:** In this questionnaire, the fiscal year is defined by how **your company** defines its fiscal year.

2. In what year did your company **first file** an annual report, such as a Form 10-K or Form 20-F, with the Securities and Exchange Commission (SEC)?

   ○ Before fiscal year 2007
   ○ During fiscal year 2007
   ○ During fiscal year 2008
   ○ During fiscal year 2009
   ○ During fiscal year 2010
   ○ During fiscal year 2011
   ○ During fiscal year 2012
   ○ No response

3. Which best describes your company?

   ○ A U.S. issuer
   ○ A foreign private issuer
   ○ No response

> **Please note:** For question 4, total market capitalization is the dollar amount of the total number of shares outstanding (non-affiliates and affiliates) multiplied by the share price.

4. What is your company's total market capitalization as of the most recently ended fiscal year?

   $ [   ]

Section 2 - Fiscal Year and Filing Status

5. What is the end date of the fiscal year for which you last filed a Form 10-K or 20-F or 40-F?
(Please enter month, day, and year. For example, if your company's fiscal year ended on December 31, 2011, and it filed its Form 10-K in February 2012, you would enter December 31, 2011.)

Month	Day	Year
[none]	[none]	[none]

6. On Form 10-K or 20-F, which box for SEC registrant filing status did your company check for each of the following fiscal years? *(Select one answer in each row.)*

	Large accelerated filer	Accelerated filer	Non-accelerated filer	Small reporting company	Not sure	Not applicable
FY 2004	○	○	○	○	○	○
FY 2005	○	○	○	○	○	○
FY 2006	○	○	○	○	○	○
FY 2007	○	○	○	○	○	○
FY 2008	○	○	○	○	○	○
FY 2009	○	○	○	○	○	○
FY 2010	○	○	○	○	○	○
FY 2011	○	○	○	○	○	○
FY 2012	○	○	○	○	○	○

> **Please note:** Throughout this questionnaire, ICFR will refer to "internal control over financial reporting."

7. In which of the following fiscal years did your company have an independent audit of the effectiveness of its ICFR? *(Select one answer in each row.)*

	Yes	No	Not sure	Not applicable
FY 2004	○	○	○	○
FY 2005	○	○	○	○
FY 2006	○	○	○	○
FY 2007	○	○	○	○
FY 2008	○	○	○	○
FY 2009	○	○	○	○
FY 2010	○	○	○	○
FY 2011	○	○	○	○
FY 2012	○	○	○	○

8. Which one of the following statements best describes your company?

○ We have always been a non-accelerated filer or a smaller reporting company

○ We were once a non-accelerated filer or a smaller reporting company, but are no longer a non-accelerated filer or small reporting company

○ We were once a large accelerated filer or accelerated filer, but are no longer a large accelerated filer
or accelerated filer

○ We have always been a large accelerated filer or accelerated filer *(Click here to go to Section 3 - Total
Audit Fees)*

○ Not sure *(Click here to go to Section 3 - Total Audit Fees)*

8a. Did your company ever **voluntarily** have an independent audit of the effectiveness of its ICFR?

　　○ Yes - *Continue with question 8b.*

　　○ No *(Click here to skip to question 8e)*

　　○ Not sure *(Click here to skip to question 8e)*

8b. For which of the following reason(s) did your company choose to voluntarily have an independent
audit of the effectiveness of its ICFR? *(Select all that apply.)*

　　☐ To evaluate the effectiveness of the company's internal controls

　　☐ To instill audit committee confidence in the company's ICFR

　　☐ To ensure the quality of the company's financial reporting

　　☐ To improve company's ability to raise capital

　　☐ To instill investor confidence in the company

　　☐ To detect or prevent potential fraud

　　☐ For other reason(s) - *If selected, specify other reason(s) below.*

| Please specify other reason(s): | |

8c. Since fiscal year 2004 has your company ever **stopped having a voluntary audit** of the
effectiveness of its ICFR?

　　○ Yes - *Continue with 8d.*

　　○ No *(Click here to skip to question 8e)*

　　○ Not sure *(Click here to skip to question 8e)*

8d. *(If yes)* For what reason(s) did your company choose to stop having a voluntary audit of the
effectiveness of its ICFR? *(Select all that apply.)*

　　☐ We no longer qualified for an exemption from an audit of the ICFR

　　☐ They are too costly

　　☐ They are too time-consuming

　　☐ We believe it was useful to do once but not on an annual basis

　　☐ We believe that non-accelerated filers and smaller reporting companies should be exempt from
this requirement

　　☐ For other reason(s) - *If selected, specify other reason(s) below.*

| Please specify other reason(s): | |

8e. For the next fiscal year, does your company plan to voluntarily have an independent audit of the
effectiveness its ICFR?

　　○ Yes *(Click here to go to Section 3 - Total Audit Fees)*

　　○ No - *Continue with question 8f.*

　　○ Not sure *(Click here to go to Section 3 - Total Audit Fees)*

8f. *(If no)* For what reason(s) does your company **not** plan to have a voluntary audit of the
effectiveness of its ICFR for the next fiscal year? *(Select all that apply.)*

　　☐ We no longer qualified for an exemption from an audit of the ICFR

　　☐ They are too costly

　　☐ They are too time-consuming

☐ We believe it was useful to do once but not on an annual basis
☐ We believe that non-accelerated filers and smaller reporting companies should be exempt from this requirement
☐ For other reason(s) - *If selected, specify other reason(s) below.*

Please specify other reason(s):

Section 3 - Total Audit Fees

This next section of the survey is about the total fees your company paid its independent auditor for both the audit of the financial statements and the audit of ICFR, as well as factors that may have caused those fees to change from year to year.

You should **exclude** from your total audit fees any fees paid for non-audit services (such as tax compliance services or audit services that are not related to filings of your company's financial statements with the SEC, such as fees to audit an employee benefit plan).

9. What is the **total amount of audit fees paid** to your independent auditor and the **approximate amount of fees paid for the audit of ICFR** for fiscal years 2009, 2010, 2011, and 2012? *(Enter whole dollar amounts. If unknown, check box.)*

	Total audit fees	**Approximate fees for audit of the ICFR**	
FY 2009	$ _____	$ _____	☐ Unknown
FY 2010	$ _____	$ _____	☐ Unknown
FY 2011	$ _____	$ _____	☐ Unknown
FY 2012	$ _____	$ _____	☐ Unknown

10. **For fiscal year 2011**, if the following events or factors occurred, what impact did they have on your company's total audit fees (relative to what these fees would have been had these events or factors not occurred)? *(Select one answer in each row.)*

Event or factor

	Not applicable, event did not occur	Caused higher fees	Had little or no impact	Caused lower fees	Not sure
a. Material acquisition or divestiture	○	○	○	○	○
b. Restatement of company's prior financial statements	○	○	○	○	○
c. Change in use by your independent auditor of the work of others (e.g., management, internal audit)	○	○	○	○	○
d. Adoption of new accounting and auditing pronouncements (separate from Auditing Standard No. 5)	○	○	○	○	○
e. Change of auditor	○	○	○	○	○
f. Change in the number of hours the auditor needed to conduct the audit due to changes other than those listed above	○	○	○	○	○
g. Other event or factor - *If applicable, specify other event/factor below.*	○	○	○	○	○
h. Other event or factor - *If applicable, specify other event/factor below.*	○	○	○	○	○

Please specify other event or factor for row g: _____

Please specify other event or factor for row h:

Section 4 - Fees Related to the ICFR Audit

In this section, we will ask questions about the costs of compliance that are associated with the independent audit of ICFR, which can be measured as dollar fees or time spent. In answering these questions, you should exclude from consideration the costs of the traditional financial statement audit.

Audit background and perception

11. **Between the fiscal year 2011 and fiscal year 2012 independent audits of your company's ICFR,** how much of an impact, if any, did the following factors have on the **amount of time spent by the independent auditor to conduct the audits**? *(Select one answer in each row.)*

	Not applicable	Caused a decrease in time spent	Had little or no impact on time spent	Caused an increase in time spent	Not sure
a. Change in the number of accounts and processes selected for audit	○	○	○	○	○
b. Change in the number of areas for which the independent auditor conducted walk-throughs	○	○	○	○	○
c. Change in the number of controls selected and/or the nature, timing, and extent of control testing by the auditor	○	○	○	○	○
d. Change in the number of company locations selected for audit	○	○	○	○	○
e. Change in the degree of the auditor's use of the work of others (e.g., management, internal audit)	○	○	○	○	○
f. Change in the number of hours the auditor needed to conduct the audit due to changes other than those listed above	○	○	○	○	○
g. Other change - *If applicable, specify other change(s) below.*	○	○	○	○	○

Please specify other change(s) for row g:

Use of COSO or other frameworks

The Committee of Sponsoring Organizations of the Treadway Commission's (COSO) Internal Control-Integrated Framework is a framework for designing and evaluating systems of internal control.

12. What internal control framework does your company primarily use to comply with Section 404(a) and 404(b) of the Sarbanes-Oxley Act?

○ COSO
○ Another framework - *If selected, identify the other framework below.* _____
○ Not sure

Please identify the other framework:

COSO's update to its 1992 Internal Control-Integrated Framework - This update is designed to describe how to evaluate internal controls in an operating and regulatory environment that is more complex than it was when the original framework was developed (Note: The updated internal control framework will not take effect until the first quarter of calendar year 2013.)

13. What impact, if any, do you expect the COSO updated internal control framework to have on the amount of time it will take to complete the independent audit of the ICFR **in fiscal year 2013**?

The COSO update will:

- ○ decrease the time greatly
- ○ decrease the time somewhat
- ○ have no effect
- ○ increase the time somewhat
- ○ increase the time greatly
- ○ Not sure

Non-labor costs

14. Approximately how much money did your company spend on software, hardware, travel, and any other **non-labor expenditure** to help you comply with Section 404(b) for fiscal years 2009, 2010, 2011, and 2012? *(Enter whole dollar amounts. If unknown or if not applicable, check the appropriate box.)*

	Approximate amount spent on software, hardware, travel, and other non-labor expenditures		
FY 2009	$ _____	☐ Unknown	☐ Not applicable
FY 2010	$ _____	☐ Unknown	☐ Not applicable
FY 2011	$ _____	☐ Unknown	☐ Not applicable
FY 2012	$ _____	☐ Unknown	☐ Not applicable

Section 5 - Use of Outside Vendors and/or Consultants

Many companies hire outside vendors and/or consultants to assist management in its evaluation of ICFR. These may include Sarbanes-Oxley Act 404 consultants or IT consultants or any other providers of goods and services that were obtained specifically to support the company's 404(a) - management's assessment of ICFR - and 404(b) - independent audit of ICFR - compliance process.

In this survey, **"outside vendors and/or consultants" do not include your company's independent auditor.**

15. For **any** of the following fiscal years - 2009, 2010, 2011, or 2012 did your company **hire an outside vendor and/or consultant** to assist management in its evaluation of ICFR?

   ○ Yes

   ○ No *(Click here to go to Section 6 - Internal Staff Costs)*

   ○ Not sure *(Click here to go to Section 6 - Internal Staff Costs)*

15a. Approximately how much money did your company spend on **fees paid to outside vendors and/or consultants** specifically to help you comply with Section 404(a) and 404(b) for fiscal years 2009, 2010, 2011, and 2012? *(Enter whole dollar amounts. If unknown or if not applicable, check the appropriate box.)*

Section 404(a)	Approximate amount of fees paid to outside vendors and/or consultants to comply with Section 404(a)		
FY 2009	$ _____	☐ Unknown	☐ Not applicable
FY 2010	$ _____	☐ Unknown	☐ Not applicable
FY 2011	$ _____	☐ Unknown	☐ Not applicable
FY 2012	$ _____	☐ Unknown	☐ Not applicable

Section 404(b)	Approximate amount of fees paid to outside vendors and/or consultants to comply with Section 404(b)		
FY 2009	$ _____	☐ Unknown	☐ Not applicable
FY 2010	$ _____	☐ Unknown	☐ Not applicable
FY 2011	$ _____	☐ Unknown	☐ Not applicable
FY 2012	$ _____	☐ Unknown	☐ Not applicable

15b. **For fiscal year 2011**, for each of the services identified below, to what extent, if at all, did your company rely on the services of outside vendors and/or consultants to help it comply with **Section 404(b)** of the independent audit of ICFR? *(Select one answer in each row.)*

	Great extent	Moderate extent	Some extent	No extent	Not sure
a. To identify risks to your company's financial reporting	○	○	○	○	○
b. To identify controls that address identified risks	○	○	○	○	○
c. To document controls identified to address risks	○	○	○	○	○
d. To gather evidence related to testing the operational effectiveness of controls	○	○	○	○	○
e. To test and evaluate the effectiveness of controls	○	○	○	○	○
f. To evaluate deficiencies identified to determine if they were significant deficiencies or material weaknesses	○	○	○	○	○
g. To develop disclosures on SEC filings related to management's assessment	○	○	○	○	○
h. To help you prepare for an independent audit of ICFR	○	○	○	○	○
i. Other services - *If applicable, specify other service(s) below.*	○	○	○	○	○

Please specify other services for row i:

Section 6 - Internal Staff Costs

The next series of questions will focus on your company's internal staff effort required to comply with Section 404(a) and 404(b).

16. For **any** of the following fiscal years - 2009, 2010, 2011, or 2012 did your company **use internal staff** to comply with Section 404(a) and 404(b)?

○ Yes

○ No *(Click here to go to Section 7 - Other Effects of Section 404(b))*

○ Not sure *(Click here to go to Section 7 - Other Effects of Section 404(b))*

16a. What was the approximate **total number of internal staff hours** your company spent on the 404(a) and 404(b) compliance process for fiscal years 2009, 2010, 2011, and 2012? *(Enter numbers. If unknown or if not applicable, check the appropriate box.)*

Section 404(a)	Approximate total internal staff hours spent on the 404(a) compliance process		
FY 2009	[ ] hours	□ Unknown	□ Not applicable
FY 2010	[ ] hours	□ Unknown	□ Not applicable
FY 2011	[ ] hours	□ Unknown	□ Not applicable
FY 2012	[ ] hours	□ Unknown	□ Not applicable

Section 404(b)	Approximate total internal staff hours spent on the 404(b) compliance process		
FY 2009	[ ] hours	□ Unknown	□ Not applicable
FY 2010	[ ] hours	□ Unknown	□ Not applicable
FY 2011	[ ] hours	□ Unknown	□ Not applicable
FY 2012	[ ] hours	□ Unknown	□ Not applicable

16b. **What was the approximate cost for the work done by your company's internal staff** on the 404(a) and 404(b) compliance process for fiscal years 2009, 2010, 2011, and 2012? *(Enter whole dollar amounts. If unknown or if not applicable, check the appropriate box.)*

Section 404(a)	Approximate cost for the work done by your company's internal staff on the 404(a) compliance process		
FY 2009	$ [ ]	☐ Unknown	☐ Not applicable
FY 2010	$ [ ]	☐ Unknown	☐ Not applicable
FY 2011	$ [ ]	☐ Unknown	☐ Not applicable
FY 2012	$ [ ]	☐ Unknown	☐ Not applicable

Section 404(b)	Approximate cost for the work done by your company's internal staff on the 404(b) compliance process		
FY 2009	$ [ ]	☐ Unknown	☐ Not applicable
FY 2010	$ [ ]	☐ Unknown	☐ Not applicable
FY 2011	$ [ ]	☐ Unknown	☐ Not applicable
FY 2012	$ [ ]	☐ Unknown	☐ Not applicable

Section 7 - Other Effects of Section 404(b)

We are interested in understanding the general impact that complying with Section 404(b) has had on your company and its participation in the capital markets.

17. **Whether or not your company is currently subject to complying with Section 404(b) of the Sarbanes-Oxley Act**, to the best of your knowledge, has complying with Section 404(b) had a positive impact, no impact, or a negative impact on each of the following? *(Select one answer in each row.)*

	Very positive impact	Somewhat positive impact	No impact	Somewhat negative impact	Very negative impact	Not sure
a. The quality of your company's internal control structure	○	○	○	○	○	○
b. The audit committee's confidence in the company's ICFR	○	○	○	○	○	○
c. The quality of your company's financial reporting	○	○	○	○	○	○
d. Your company's ability to prevent and detect fraud	○	○	○	○	○	○
e. Your company's ability to raise capital	○	○	○	○	○	○
f. Investor confidence in your company	○	○	○	○	○	○
g. Efficiency of your company's operation	○	○	○	○	○	○
h. The efficiency of your company's financial reporting process	○	○	○	○	○	○
i. The liquidity of your company's common stock	○	○	○	○	○	○
j. The timeliness of your company financial statement audit	○	○	○	○	○	○
k. Your company's overall firm value	○	○	○	○	○	○
l. Your confidence in the financial reports of other 404(b) compliant companies	○	○	○	○	○	○
m. Other aspect- *If applicable, specify other aspects(s) below.*	○	○	○	○	○	○

Please specify other aspects for row m: _____

Section 8 - Opinion on Costs and Benefits of Section 404(b)

18. Based on your experience complying with Section 404(b) of the Sarbanes-Oxley Act, do you think the benefits of complying with Section 404(b) outweigh the costs or do the costs outweigh the benefits?

- ○ The benefits greatly outweigh costs
- ○ The benefits somewhat outweigh the costs
- ○ The benefits and costs are about equal
- ○ The costs somewhat outweigh the benefits
- ○ The costs greatly outweigh the benefits
- ○ Not sure *(Click here to skip to question 20)*

19. What reason(s) led you to the way you answered question 18?

Section 8 - Opinion on Disclosure

20. In your opinion, should issuers that are **exempted** from the 404(b) requirement - to have an independent audit of their ICFR - **be required** to disclose the lack of such an audit to investors such as through a check box disclosure on the front of the Form 10-K?

   ○ Definitely yes
   ○ Probably yes
   ○ No opinion
   ○ Probably no
   ○ Definitely no

21. What reason(s) led you to the way you answered question 20?

Section 10 - Comments and Final Response Submission

22. If you have any additional comments regarding any previous question or any topic covered in this questionnaire, please enter them in the space below.

23. **Are you ready to submit your final completed survey to GAO?**

(This is equivalent to mailing a completed paper survey to us. It tells us that your answers are official and final.)

○ Yes, my survey is complete - *To submit your final responses, please click on "Exit" below.*

◉ No, my survey is not yet complete - *To save your responses for later, please click on "Exit" below.*

You may view and print your completed survey by clicking on the Summary link in the menu to the left.

Thank you very much for your assistance.

| Print |
| Exit |

Appendix IV: GAO Contact and Staff Acknowledgments

GAO Contact	A. Nicole Clowers, (202) 512-8678 or clowersa@gao.gov
Staff Acknowledgments	In addition to the contact named above, Karen Tremba, (Assistant Director), James Ashley, Bethany Benitez, William Chatlos, Janet Eackloff, Joe Hunter, Cathy Hurley, Stuart Kaufman, Marc Molino, Lauren Nunnally, Jennifer Schwartz, and Seyda Wentworth made key contributions to this report.

GAO-13-582 Auditor Attestation on Internal Controls

Bibliography

Studies

Alexander, C. R., S. W. Bauguess, G. Bernile, Y. A. Lee, and J. Marietta-Westberg. "The Economic Effects of SOX Section 404 Compliance: A Corporate Insider Perspective." Working paper. March 2010.

Asare, S. K., and A. Wright. "The Effect of Type of Internal Control Report on Users' Confidence in the Accompanying Financial Statement Audit Report." *Contemporary Accounting Research*, vol. 29, no. 1 (2012).

Ashbaugh-Skaife, H., D. Collins, W. Kinney, and R. LaFond. "The Effect of Internal Control Deficiencies on Firm Risk and Cost of Equity." *Journal of Accounting Research*, vol. 47, no. 1 (2009).

Audit Analytics. "2011 Financial Restatements: An Eleven Year Comparison." Sutton, Mass.: 2012.

Audit Analytics, "2009 Financial Restatements: A Nine Year Comparison." (Sutton, Mass.: February 2010).

Audit Analytics. "Restatements Disclosed by the Two Types of SOX 404 Issuers: (1) Auditor Attestation Filers and (2) Management-Only Report Filers." Sutton, Mass.: November 2009.

Brown, K., P. Pacharn, J. Li, E. Mohammad, F. A. Elayan, and F. Chu. "The Valuation Effect and Motivations of Voluntary Compliance with Auditor's Attestation Under Sarbanes-Oxley Act Section 404 (B)." Working paper. January 15, 2012.

Cassell, C.A., L. A. Myers, and J. Zhou. "The Effects of Voluntary Internal Control Audits on the Cost of Capital." Working paper. February 13, 2013.

Chief Financial Officers' Council and the President's Council on Integrity and Efficiency, *Estimating the Costs and Benefits of Rendering an Opinion on Internal Control over Financial Reporting.*

Coates IV, J. C. "The Goals and Promise of the Sarbanes-Oxley Act." *Journal of Economic Perspective*, vol. 21, no. 1 (2007).

Crabtree, A., and J. J. Mahler. "Credit ratings, Cost of Debt, and Internal Control Disclosures: A Comparison of SOX 302 and SOX 404." *The Journal of Applied Business Research*, vol. 28, no. 5 (2012).

Dhaliwal, D., C. Hogan, R. Trezevant, and M. Wilkins. "Internal Control Disclosures, Monitoring, and the Cost of Debt." *The Accounting Review*, vol. 86, no. 4 (2011).

GAO. *Community Banks and Credit Unions: Impact of the Dodd-Frank Act Depends Largely on Future Rule Makings.* GAO-12-881. Washington, D.C.: September 13, 2012.

GAO. *Financial Restatements: Update of Public Company Trends, Market Impacts, and Regulatory Enforcement Activities.* GAO-06-678. Washington, D.C.: March 5, 2007.

GAO. *Sarbanes-Oxley Act: Consideration of Key Principles Needed in Addressing Implementation for Smaller Public Companies.* GAO-06-361. Washington, D.C.: April 13, 2006.

Holder, A. D., K. E. Karim, and A. Robin. "Was Dodd-Frank Justified in Exempting Small Firms from Section 404b Compliance?" *Accounting Horizons*, vol. 27, no. 1 (2013).

Iliev, P. "The Effect of SOX Section 404: Costs, Earnings Quality, and Stock Prices." *Journal of Finance*, vol. 65, no. 3 (2010).

Kim, J. B., B. Y. Song, and L. Zhang. "The Internal Control Weakness and Bank Loan Contracting: Evidence from SOX Section 404 Disclosures." *The Accounting Review*, vol. 86, no. 4 (2011).

Kinney, W. R., and M. L. Shepardson. "Do Control Effectiveness Disclosures Require SOX 404(b) Internal Control Audits?: A Natural Experiment with Small U.S. Public Companies." *Journal of Accounting Research*, vol. 49, no. 2 (2011).

Krishnan, G.V., and W. Yu. "Do Small Firms Benefit from Auditor Attestation of Internal Control Effectiveness?" *Auditing: A Journal of Practice and Theory*, vol. 34, no. 4 (2012).

Nagy, A. L. "Section 404 Compliance and Financial Reporting Quality." *Accounting Horizons*, vol. 24, no. 3 (2010).

Orcutt, J. L. "The Case Against Exempting Smaller Reporting Companies from Sarbanes-Oxley Section 404: Why Market-Based Solutions are Likely to Harm Ordinary Investors." *Fordham Journal of Corporate and Financial Law*, vol. 14, no. 2 (2009).

Schneider, A., A. Gramling, D. R. Hermanson, and Z. Ye. "A Review of Academic Literature on Internal Control Reporting Under SOX." *Journal of Accounting Literature*, vol. 28 (2009).

Schneider, A., and B. K. Church. "The Effect of Auditors' Internal Control Opinions on Loan Decisions." *Journal of Accounting and Public Policy*, vol. 27, no.1 (2008).

Scholz, Susan. *The Changing Nature and Consequences of Public Company Financial Restatements: 1997-2006*. A special report prepared at the request of the Department of the Treasury. April 2008.

U.S. Securities and Exchange Commission. *Study and Recommendations on Section 404(b) of the Sarbanes-Oxley Act of 2002 For Issuers with Public Float Between $75 and $250 Million*. Washington, D.C.: 2011.

U.S. Securities and Exchange Commission. *Study of the Sarbanes-Oxley Act of 2002 Section 404 Internal Control over Financial Reporting Requirements*. Washington, D.C.: 2009.

Surveys

Center for Audit Quality. *The CAQ's Sixth Annual Main Street Investor Survey*, September 2012.

Center for Audit Quality. *The CAQ's Fourth Annual Individual Investor*, September 2010.

Financial Executives International and Financial Executives Research Foundation, *2012 Audit Fee Survey*. Morristown, N.J.: 2012.

Financial Executives International and Financial Executives Research Foundation, *Special Survey on Sarbanes-Oxley Section 404 Implementation*. Morristown, N.J.: 2005.

PCAOB. *2012 SOX Compliance Survey: Role, Relevancy and Value of the Audit*. 2012.

Protiviti, *2013 Sarbanes-Oxley Compliance Survey: Building Value in Your SOX Compliance Program*. 2013.

Protiviti, *2012 Sarbanes-Oxley Compliance Survey: Where U.S.-Listed Companies Stand – Reviewing Cost, Time, Effort and Process*. 2012.